# ACTION RESEARCH
# IN HIGHER EDUCATION

# ACTION RESEARCH IN HIGHER EDUCATION

## Examples and Reflections

Ortrun Zuber-Skerritt

KOGAN
PAGE

First published in 1992

Apart from any fair dealing for the purposes of research or private study, or criticism or review, as permitted under the Copyright, Designs and Patents Act, 1988, this publication may only be reproduced stored or transmitted, in any form or by any means, with the prior permission in writing of the publishers, or in the case of reprographic reproduction in accordance with the terms of licences issued by the Copyright Licensing Agency. Enquiries concerning reproduction outside those terms should be sent the the publishers at the undermentioned address:

Kogan Page Limited
120 Pentonville Road
London N1 9JN

© Ortrun Zuber-Skerritt 1992

**British Library Cataloguing in Publication Data**
A CIP record for this book is available from the British Library.

ISBN 0 7494 0741 7

Printed and bound in Great Britain by Biddles Ltd, Guildford

Cover design by Teresa Jablonski representing continuous cyclical movement ◄— in a process of six major stages ☐ ☐ :  problem and needs analysis; strategic planning; action, i.e. implementation of the strategic plan; observation and evaluation; reflection on the evaluation of results; identification of new problems and needs; etc.

# Contents

## PART I:   ACTION RESEARCH IN HIGHER EDUCATION

## PART II:   EXAMPLES OF ACTION RESEARCH

# PART III:  REFLECTIONS ON ACTION RESEARCH

# List of tables

# List of figures

# List of abbreviations

| | |
|---|---|
| CALAR | Centre for Action Learning and Action Research |
| CALT | Centre for the Advancement of Learning and Teaching |
| CMP | Coursework Master Programme |
| CRASP | Critical attitude, Research into teaching, Accountability, Self-evaluation, Professionalism |
| ESRC | Economic and Social Research Council |
| EUT | Excellence in University Teaching |
| HE | higher education |
| HERDSA | Higher Education Research and Development Society of Australia |
| MAS | School of Modern Asian Studies |
| SERC | Science and Engineering Research Council |
| SLS | student learning skills |
| SU | semester unit |
| UK | United Kingdom |
| US | United States of America |

# Acknowledgements

I acknowledge the kind permission of the editors to reprint parts of previously published studies listed in the References as Zuber-Skerritt (1986a; 1987b; 1990b;1991 ).

I appreciate the collaboration of my colleagues at Griffith University, especially those with whom I have co-authored articles, material from which is reproduced with their permission in Chapter 3.

I am also grateful to the staff in the CVCP/USDTU, based at Sheffield University, for their assistance with typing and wordprocessing.

Finally I wish to thank Sue Jarvis for proofreading, and Teresa Jablonski and Terry Wood for design and layout, and for compiling the indexes.

*Ortrun Zuber-Skerritt, 1992*

# Foreword

Although I have been working for over 50 years with managers of coalmines, with presidents of international banks, with doctors running London's biggest hospitals, with Third Worlders in charge of national corporations and of village workshops, with adolescents successful in purging vandalism from their schools and with police aware that ethnic violence has lessons for us all and, although my writings on all this (and much more besides) have been identified as 'the best book that has been written so far on management education'* , I am quite ready to believe that either, or both, of Ortrun Zuber-Skerritt's current works might lead my friendly critic to have his reservations.

While my own work might have described what had been studied in many different cultures as to how many very different kinds of activity were managed, it merely reflects what I myself imagined was going on. Dr Zuber-Skerritt compares and contrasts the work of others. Since all truths are but half-truths, such comparisons and contrasts may help us all to ask if there ever was and ever could be such a thing as 'the best book' — by whomsoever claims to be its author?

*Reg Revans*

*Professor Emeritus*
*Manchester, 1992*

---

* Weeks, B. (1984) Action key to managerial learning, *Management Review*, February.

# Introduction

## Aims of the book

This book has arisen from my work with academics and students in higher education whose aim it was to improve their practice, skill and conditions of learning and teaching. Its purpose is to present a series of case studies in higher education which demonstrate how teams of academics — in collaboration with their staff development colleagues — have:

1. improved the practice of learning, teaching and professional development;
2. advanced knowledge in higher education by generating 'grounded theory' (Glaser and Strauss, 1967), research and publications; and
3. documented excellent teaching.

It is *not* the aim of this book to provide and claim generalisable 'objective truth', nor to present a large-scale statistical survey and an extensive evaluation of the literature on improving learning and teaching, nor to predict future trends and behavioural practices in higher education.

Rather, the aim is to describe processes and procedures used in a particular educational setting and to distil those principles and 'grounded' theories (Glaser and Strauss, 1967) which have emerged from collaborative enquiry by higher education teachers into their practice in this particular context.

The methodology used is *action research*. This may be defined as collaborative, critical enquiry by the academics themselves (rather than expert educational researchers) into their own teaching practice, into

1

problems of student learning and into curriculum problems. It is professional development through academic course development, group reflection, action, evaluation and improved practice.

The book will be of interest to staff developers and teachers in higher education and any people who are interested in improving learning and teaching, as well as in conceptualising these innovative processes and publishing the results. The advantages of publishing the results of action research in refereed journals are that these publications not only document the authors' excellence in teaching and their research achievements, but also contribute to their institution's accountability. This legitimises action research in higher education which integrates theory and practice, teaching and research; it is thus a way to true professionalism.

## The nature of action research

Limerick (1991) says in his Foreword to my book *Action Research for Change and Development*:

> Action research as a concept, a philosophy and a methodology of learning has arrived... What has been for many years a trickle of protest at conventional research and learning methods has become a major stream of thought which is attracting a great deal of attention in Australia and overseas... The new operation of collaborative individuals capable of bringing down the Berlin Wall was hardly likely to tolerate the implacable imperatives of institutionalised education. They found an alternative in the emancipatory processes of action research.

Action research means different things to different people. Some are very demanding and exclusive in their definition of what does and does not count as action research. Others use the term loosely, perhaps even to cover up shoddy research or a lack of ability to do scientific research.

This book tries to contribute to the legitimacy of action research in higher education by providing a description of its features and basic requirements (Chapter 1), examples of improved practice at the undergraduate level (Chapter 2) and at the postgraduate level (Chapter 3), a methodology which is particularly useful in action research for identifying and negotiating people's constructs of teaching, research and professional development (Chapter 4) and by providing evidence that action research is one of the most effective methods of professional development (Chapter 5). The book ends with meta-action research, that is, my action research into the action research presented in the previous chapters (Chapter 6). The following is an overview of the structure and the content of the book, with a brief summary of each chapter.

## Overview of the book

The book is structured in three main parts: action research in higher education (Chapter 1), examples of action research (Chapters 2–4) and reflections on action research (Chapters 5–6).

*Chapter 1* is a concise description of the characteristics of action research and of some of the theoretical assumptions underlying the processes and procedures. It also provides a justification of action research, and reasons why it is particularly appropriate, in higher education. This CRASP model (**C**ritical attitude, **R**esearch into teaching, **A**ccountability, **S**elf-evaluation, **P**rofessionalism) and the theoretical framework for action research discussed in more detail in the companion book (*Professional Development in Higher Education — A Theoretical Framework for Action Research,* 1992). The main purpose of this present book is to present examples of and reflections about improving the practice of learning and teaching in higher education.

*Chapter 2* argues that student learning skills need to be developed systematically (rather than accidentally) by the teachers in higher education themselves (rather than by outside experts) and integrated into students' academic programmes as a normal, ongoing (rather than remedial) learning activity. A case study at Griffith University is discussed in which students' experiences confirmed the research-based principles of student 'learning by discovery' and 'through discussion', of 'problem-solving' and a 'deep meaning approach to learning'. The study involved the integration of workshops on student learning skills and problem-solving into a first-year programme. Although this learning skills programme has been designed specifically in response to students' problems and needs at Griffith University, it can be readily translated and adapted to the educational context of other higher education institutions.

*Chapter 3* argues for the systematic development and integration of student research skills in postgraduate programmes. Case studies from Griffith University, arising from action research projects with university teachers, illustrate five strategies:

1.  the review of a postgraduate programme, identifying student problems and a gap between institutional expectations and students' needs;
2.  the workshop model for developing skills in dissertation research and writing;

3. the focus on two key problem areas in the process of writing a thesis;
4. the design, implementation and evaluation of a course on 'Problems and Methods in Research' for the beginning researcher in the social sciences as an alternative model and supplement to the single-supervisor model in postgraduate education; and
5. student metacognition and learning how to research through eliciting some changing personal constructs of research effectiveness.

There has been little educational research and development in postgraduate education. This chapter explores some of the issues and problems identified at Griffith University and elsewhere. Our methods may be adapted by other higher education institutions to their particular educational context.

*Chapter 4* introduces a research methodology in higher education which enables us to elicit personal theories of several aspects of higher education (e.g. research, teaching and professional development) and which is an alternative to the traditional methods of studying people's perceptions and perspectives (e.g. by questionnaire, interview or structured group discussion). The chapter outlines Kelly's repertory grid technique and the theoretical assumptions on which the technique is based. Some examples are given to illustrate how this research method may be applied to higher education research and development and how it may assist people to reconstrue their teaching or research practice.

*Chapter 5* uses the repertory grid technology to elicit personal constructs of professional development from those academics who participated in the action research projects described in Chapters 2 and 3, as well as in other kinds of staff development activities. The results are significant in that they confirm my thesis that action research as defined in this book is the most effective method of professional development.

*Chapter 6* is about my own reflections as a consultant in higher education. These concern the nature of action research in relation:

1. to student learning about their own learning in an academic course or programme;
2. to staff learning about student learning; and
3. to my own learning about both of these areas.

To relate this chapter to the main arguments in the companion book (Zuber-Skerritt, 1992), references to theories or principles are provided as 'advance organisers' (in brief key terms and indicated in italics and brackets). Other references — for example, to the case studies in this book — are also given (in brackets, but in normal type). This chapter reflects my action research on action research projects, using case study methodology and following the structure of *The Action Research Planner* (Kemmis and McTaggart, 1982).

## Two inter-related but independent publications

Whilst this volume on *Action Research in Higher Education — Examples and Reflections* and the companion book on *Professional Development in Higher Education — A Theoretical Framework for Action Research* are conceived as one coherent entity, some readers might only be interested in the practice, and others in the theory of learning, teaching and staff development in higher education. Hence the work is presented in two separate volumes.

## Action research network

People interested in being kept informed about further developments in action research in higher education may join the network of the recently established international Centre for Action Learning and Action Research (CALAR), Division of Commerce and Administration, Griffith University, Brisbane, Qld, 4111, Australia (see Figure 1).

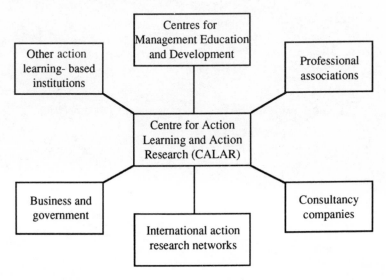

**Figure 1** *CALAR network*

# PART I

# ACTION RESEARCH IN HIGHER EDUCATION

# Chapter 1

# Action research for improving and advancing learning and teaching

## Introduction

The general assumption and common practice has been to regard educational theory as being created by educational researchers and applied by some practitioners in higher education (HE). Despite the extensive literature on student learning and adult education, lectures and final examinations are still the most frequently used methods in HE. Although educational theory has contributed a great deal to the advancement of knowledge in higher education over the past two decades or more, it has not made a significant impact on learning and teaching *practice* in HE. Most academics are unaware of recent theories, principles and methods of learning and teaching. In general, they do not read books or journal articles on higher education, partly because of their greater emphasis on research priorities in their own disciplines, partly because of the jargon used in most educational and psychological research papers, which is alien to practitioners, and possibly for other reasons.

I am not suggesting, however, that it is the frailty of educational theory or theorists that should necessarily be made responsible for the lack of impact on higher education practice, or that the species of educational researchers should be altogether wiped out and replaced by practitioners doing action research. Rather, I suggest that action research is not only a possible alternative to advancing knowledge in higher education; it is also a more effective and immediate way of improving HE learning and teaching practice.

Many teachers in higher education want to improve their teaching (Moses, 1985a). They may attend staff development sessions or they may consult the literature in the field and/or an educational adviser. In most cases, they usually expect a quick answer to their question or problem, an easy formula or recipe for applying the 'right' strategy according to 'expert' researchers and based on established theory and educational technology. This technocratic approach to improving teaching in higher education, that is, applying theories (generated by educational researchers), principles and techniques to one's own practice, is analogical to the 'reproducing' or 'surface' approach taken by students to learning and studying (i.e. acquiring factual knowledge and skills from books and lectures by memorising and reproducing them in examinations).

Although the technology of improving teaching 'techniques' and student study 'skills' has been developed to a fine art and applied effectively in many ways, the case studies mentioned in this volume suggest that a more appropriate approach to HE learning and teaching might be a 'deep-meaning' orientation (i.e. trying to understand the idea and meaning of a discourse; relating them to one's own existing knowledge; and being able to transfer the acquired knowledge and skills to new situations), problem-solving, experiential learning and learning by discovery (e.g. in small-group discussions). It is in these active and creative learning situations that theoretical knowledge can be generated by the participants themselves and that generative learning and action research by practitioners into their own practice may advance knowledge in that field. This claim is evidenced by the fact that the case studies referred to in this volume have all been accepted as papers at national and international conferences, as book chapters or articles in refereed journals, such as *Higher Education* (UK), *Higher Education Research and Development* (Australia), *Zeitschrift für Hochschuldidaktik* (Austria) and *Qualitative Studies in Education* (US).

The purpose of this chapter is to provide a brief overview of the conceptual framework and methodology of action research applied to the case studies in this book on improving practice in higher education. This is achieved by outlining the nature (aims, processes, basic assumptions and characteristics) of action research followed by a general description and discussion of the processes and procedures of the case studies.

## The nature of action research

The relationship between research and action, between theory and practice, is often conceived as a dichotomy. In higher education, academics consider themselves either as educational researchers/theorists or as practising teachers. However, there is an emerging paradigm in the social sciences that recognises the dialectical relationship between theory and practice. For a more detailed discussion see Zuber-Skerritt (1992).

Action research reflects this dialectic (i.e. action and research are like two sides of a coin). Action and practical experience may be the foundations of educational research, and research may inform practice and lead to action. Academics are in an ideal position; on the one side they can create and advance knowledge in higher education on the basis of their concrete, practical experience; on the other side, they can actively improve practice on the basis of their 'grounded theory'.

Carr and Kemmis (1986) distinguish between three types of action research which I have summarised in Table 1.

For Carr and Kemmis only emancipatory action research is true action research. In my view the three types are developmental stages, and it is quite legitimate to start with technical enquiry and progressively develop through practical to emancipatory action research. However, the ultimate aim should be to improve practice in a systematic way and, if warranted, to suggest and make changes to the environment, context or conditions in which that practice takes place, and which impede desirable improvement and effective future development.

The process of action research was first conceptualised by Lewin (1952) and further developed by Kolb (1984), Carr and Kemmis (1986) and others. In brief, it is a spiral of cycles of action and research consisting of four major moments: *plan, act, observe* and *reflect* (Figure 2).

The plan includes problem analysis and a strategic plan; action refers to the implementation of the strategic plan; observation includes an evaluation of the action by appropriate methods and techniques; and reflection means reflecting on the results of the evaluation and on the whole action and research process, which may lead to the identification of a new problem or problems and hence a new cycle of planning, acting, observing and reflecting.

The basic assumption is that people can learn and create knowledge:

1. on the basis of their concrete experience;
2. through observing and reflecting on that experience;

11

**Table 1** *Types of action research and their main characteristics (after Carr and Kemmis, 1986)*

| Type of action research | Aims | Facilitator's role | Relationship between facilitator and participants |
|---|---|---|---|
| 1. Technical | Effectiveness/ efficiency of educational practice Professional development | Outside 'expert' | Co-option (of practitioners who depend on facilitator) |
| 2. Practical | As (1) above Practitioners' understanding Transformation of their consciousness | Socratic role, encouraging participation and self-reflection | Co-operation (process consultancy) |
| 3. Emancipatory | As (2) above Participants' emancipation from the dictates of tradition, self-deception, coercion Their critique of bureaucratic systematisation Transformation of the organisation and of the educational system | Process moderator (responsibility shared equally by participants) | Collaboration |

3. by forming abstract concepts and generalisations; and
4. by testing the implications of these concepts in new situations, which will lead to new concrete experience and hence to the beginning of a new cycle (Figure 3).

Action research is an alternative approach to traditional social science research in that it is:

- *practical.* The results and insights gained from the research are not only of theoretical importance to the advancement of knowledge in the field, but also lead to practical improvements during and after the research process.
- *participative and collaborative.* The researcher is not considered to be an outside expert conducting an enquiry with

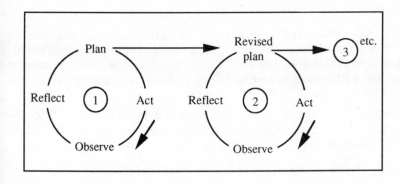

**Figure 2** *The traditional spiral of action research cycles*

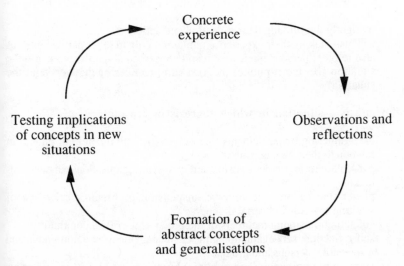

**Figure 3** *The Lewinian experiential learning model (Kolb, 1984, 21)*

'subjects', but a co-worker doing research with and for the people concerned with the practical problem and its actual improvement.
- *emancipatory.* The approach is not hierarchical; rather, all people concerned are equal 'participants' contributing to the enquiry.
- *interpretive.* Social enquiry is not assumed to result in the researcher's positivist statements based on right or wrong answers to the research question, but in solutions based on the views and interpretations of the people involved in the enquiry. Research validity is achieved by certain methods.

13

- *critical.* The 'critical community' of participants not only search for practical improvements in their work within the given socio-political constraints, but also act as critical and self-critical change agents of those constraints. They change their environment and are changed in the process.

Table 2 presents the working definition jointly authored by the participants at the International Symposium on Action Research, Brisbane, March 1989.

**Table 2** *Working definition of action research*

**If yours is a situation in which**

- people reflect and improve (or develop) their *own* work and their *own* situations
- by tightly interlinking their reflection and action
- and also making their experience public not only to other participants but also to other persons interested in and concerned about the work and the situation (i.e. their (public) theories and practices of the work and the situation)

**and if yours is a situation in which there is increasingly**

- data-gathering by participants themselves (or with the help of others) in relation to their own questions
- participation (in problem-posing and in answering questions) in decision-making
- power-sharing and the relative suspension of hierarchical ways of working towards industrial democracy
- collaboration among members of the group as a 'critical community'
- self-reflection, self-evaluation and self-management by autonomous and responsible persons and groups
- learning progressively (and publicly) by doing and by making mistakes in a 'self-reflective spiral' of planning, acting, observing, reflecting, replanning, etc.
- reflection which supports the idea of the '(self-) reflective practitioner'

**then** yours is a situation in which ACTION RESEARCH is occurring.

## The CRASP model

My own way of describing action research is by the acronym CRASP in Table 3.

**Table 3**  *The CRASP model of action research*

Action research is:

*Critical* (and self-critical) collaborative enquiry by
*Reflective* practitioners being
*Accountable* and making the results of their enquiry public,
*Self-evaluating* their practice and engaged in
*Participative* problem-solving and continuing professional development.

Kemmis and his associates have argued for, and successfully introduced, action research in teacher training at the primary and secondary levels. At the higher education level action research is not only possible, but particularly appropriate for at least five reasons which may be again summarised in the acronym CRASP: *Action research promotes a Critical attitude, Research into teaching, Accountability, Self-evaluation and Professionalism,* all of which are important university goals, not only in Australia, but anywhere in the world. These goals have been stated and demanded frequently in recent years, but they have not been achieved satisfactorily, because they are difficult to put into practice. Action research may provide a practical solution to this problem. Through systematic, controlled action research, higher education teachers can become more professional, more interested in pedagogical aspects of higher education and more motivated to integrate their research and teaching interests in a holistic way. This, in turn, can lead to greater job satisfaction, better academic programmes, improvement of student learning and practitioners' insights and contributions to the advancement of knowledge in higher education.

The main benefits of action research are the improvement of practice, the improvement of the understanding of practice by its practitioners and the improvement of the situation in which the practice takes place. In order to achieve the full potential of these gains, a single loop of action research (or 'arrested' action research) is not sufficient. What is needed is an organised process of learning or the 'organisation of enlightenment' in critical communities (Habermas, 1978), that is, the use of a spiral of action research cycles by the learning community of action researchers. The main features of this kind of action research are participation and collaboration, action-orientation, critical function, and a spiral of cycles of planning, acting, observing and reflecting (Figure 2). The participatory and collaborative character of action research is explained by Grundy and Kemmis (1988:87) as follows:

> Action research is research into practice, by practitioners, for practitioners... In action research, all actors involved in the research process are equal participants, and must be involved in every stage of the research... The kind of involvement required is collaborative involvement. It requires a special kind of communication... which has been described as 'symmetrical communication', ... which allows all participants to be partners of communication on equal terms... Collaborative participation in theoretical, practical and political discourse is thus a hallmark of action research and the action researcher.

One might argue that it is the normal, commonsense practice of every practitioner to plan, act, observe and reflect. But in action research this is done more carefully, more systematically and more rigorously than in everyday life. Kemmis and McTaggart (1982) have produced a procedural guide for teachers and administrators who are interested in improvement and change in their schools. This *Action Research Planner* can easily be adapted to action research in higher education. It provides a way of thinking systematically about what happens in the teaching practice, implementing action where improvements are considered to be possible, and monitoring and evaluating the effects of the action for continuing future improvement.

Educational researchers may stimulate, encourage and facilitate the action research process and provide relevant advice and references for the practitioners' analysis and solution of problems. The joint findings can be disseminated in educational or professional journals and conference proceedings. That this is possible to achieve in actual practice is evidenced by the following examples of published action research projects conducted at Griffith University: Zuber-Skerritt and Marwick (1976), Moss and McMillen (1980), Bridgestock and Backhouse (1982), Harris and Zuber-Skerritt (1986), Zuber-Skerritt and Knight (1985, 1986), Knight and Zuber-Skerritt (1986), Diamond and Zuber-Skerritt (1986) and Zuber-Skerritt and Rix (1986).

These case studies demonstrate how some university teachers in at least three interdisciplinary schools at one university (i.e. in the School of Modern Asian Studies, Humanities and Science and Technology at Griffith University) conducted action research projects in collaboration with academic development staff (from the Centre for the Advancement of Learning and Teaching). In general terms, the participants carried out the following action research activities:

1.   identified and analysed a problem in the curriculum;

2. designed strategies for solving the problem;
3. implemented and tested the strategies;
4. evaluated the effectiveness;
5. reflected on the results as a team;
6. arrived at conclusions and/or newly identified problems;
7. repeated this cycle again (sometimes several times) until they were satisfied with their improved practice; and finally
8. reported on their findings, usually initially in an internal report to a School Programme Committee or Board or to the Standing Committee (of the School of Modern Asian Studies); and then, in the light of this discussion and the Committee's resolutions, either repeated an action research cycle, if warranted, or wrote up a research paper, first to be presented and discussed at a conference, and then revised and submitted to a journal of higher education.

In other words, these university teachers followed the procedures of systematic action research as developed by Kemmis and his associates, who see the four fundamental moments of action research linked dynamically in a cycle: to plan, to act, to observe and to reflect. Other examples of action research in higher education are:

- introducing information technology in institutions;
- developing innovative methods in farming communities;
- changing organisational culture;
- developing managerial and supervisory competencies;
- quality improvement programmes, etc.

## Conclusion

The action research projects at Griffith University mentioned above and described in the following chapters were initiated by university teachers — as individuals, teaching teams, programme committees, convenors of a course or programme, or as members of the Standing Committee — not by external researchers. My role as a consultant in academic development can at best be described as that of a facilitator and team worker. We all contributed in various ways and learned from one another as we discussed our aims and tasks (described above in points 1-8). The co-authored publications may reflect this team spirit. They certainly were a challenging, most satisfying and enjoyable experience for all involved. They were started in order to test my theories on action research in higher education and to follow the action research process, but they turned out to have a multiplier effect in that they proved to be an incentive for several other academics who have expressed their interest in participating in action research projects.

The readers are invited to consider whether the process and outcomes of the following examples of action research are transferable to their particular situation and educational context. The studies cover the development of student learning skills at the undergraduate level (Chapter 2) and at the postgraduate level (Chapter 3), the development of people's awareness of research and teaching effectiveness (Chapter 4) and effective professional development (Chapter 5) and my own meta-action research (Chapter 6).

The next chapter explains how a teaching team at an Australian university developed and integrated a learning skills component in a first-year interdisciplinary degree programme.

# PART II

# EXAMPLES OF ACTION RESEARCH

# Chapter 2

# Helping undergraduate students learn

## Introduction

While the Australian student population in higher education used to be fairly homogeneous with regard to formal education and parental background (with a consequent homogeneity of knowledge, skills, needs and expectations), it has become more and more heterogeneous since the democratisation of, and increased open access to, higher education since the 1960s. Research studies and reports in recent years have pointed to problems of students' lack of background knowledge, basic skills and higher level skills necessary for study in higher education, and to problems of attrition, drop-out and late completion rates. Various strategies for improvement have been introduced in higher education; for example, more rigorous selection criteria and procedures in order to maintain high standards; educational research into the processes and problems of student learning; and the development of innovative strategies in order to help students overcome their problems and to help them learn and succeed in their study at all levels.

The purpose of this chapter is to contribute to the latter area of concern, that is, the improvement of student learning and — related to this — the improvement of teaching in higher education (HE) through workshop and curriculum review activities. This study has grown out of practice rather than theory. Recent theories on student learning have had some impact on HE teaching practice, either directly through academics who read books and journals in higher education (although they are, no doubt, in the minority) or indirectly through educational advisers in higher education research and development centres. However, a large percentage of academics still know little about the literature on student learning. The question to be answered is 'How can this gap between educational theory and practice be bridged?'

Rather than starting from theories on student learning and then applying them to practice, this chapter aims to show how student learning can be improved through practical considerations and changes in the curriculum by teaching academics. In other words, the chapter deals with action research on student learning. Action research is defined as the search by HE teachers themselves for solutions to problems in student learning and the testing of these solutions through evaluation, reflection on and review of the solutions found. The 'teacher as researcher' movement, or action research, focuses on practical problems arising from particular situations and aims at illuminating such situations for all the participants involved (cf Carr and Kemmis, 1986). In this chapter, student 'learning skills' are defined in the widest meaning as learning methods; strategies of learning and studying; information and retrieval skills; analytical skills; problem-solving; oral and written communication skills. Svensson (1984, 56) uses the term 'skill':

> to refer to the nature or quality of an interaction ... Instances of listening, writing and problem-solving ... can be considered to represent skills. Such skills are conditions for and parts of learning and the quality of learning is dependent upon the quality of the skills displayed.

However, Svensson (1984, 68) sees a difference between 'study skills', which 'represent relatively superficial and peripheral aspects of the activity of studying', and 'skill in studying' which he describes as 'the quality of students' performance on a study task which is embedded within a course'.

Various studies (e.g. Marton et al., 1984) demonstrate that a deep approach to learning is more effective in the long term than a surface approach, and that the intervention of a study skills programme is less effective than that of a skill-in-studying or learning-to-learn programme. Although Marton and his followers may prefer a 'pure' intervention of inducing a deep approach to learning in students (i.e. a learning-to-learn programme), an eclectic intervention might be more realistic and necessary in actual practice in order to achieve the same aim. There are two main reasons why an eclectic approach may be more acceptable to staff and students.

The first is staff attitude. Many academics do not share the implicit assumption in the research literature that a surface approach to learning is bad and should be discouraged. They usually maintain that it is necessary for students in their particular discipline to acquire a certain body of factual knowledge by rote learning, memorising and reproducing facts before they can actually start to apply these facts, or to analyse and solve problems which require factual knowledge. Yet the same academics are usually capable of, and successful in, stimulating critical and analytical thinking in their students at the same time. Their ultimate goal may be the same as that of educational researchers, that is, developing students' deep approach to learning and a high-level conception of learning, but their ways and means of reaching this goal differ. The present case study shows how this staff attitude can be accommodated and how their processes of teaching may be assisted and further stimulated by a systematic and well-designed learning skills programme. It has been implied and asserted in some educational research that the encouragement of a surface approach is detrimental to students' development of a deep approach, but this has not yet been proven. On the contrary, students seem to shift quite comfortably from one to the other approach, depending on their perceptions of assessment requirements and staff expectations (Laurillard, 1984).

The second argument for an eclectic approach to designing a learning skills programme concerns students' conceptions and needs. Adults hold different conceptions of learning which Säljö (1982) categorises into five stages:

1. learning as a quantitative increase in knowledge;
2. memorising;
3. the acquisition of facts, methods, procedures, etc.;
4. the abstraction of meaning; and
5. an interpretative process aimed at the understanding of reality.

The first three stages correspond to a surface approach; the last two to a deep approach to learning. Our experience suggests that novices to a subject or to an institution start at one of the first stages of conception, probably in order to build an information base as fast as possible for subsequent personal interpretation and understanding. This gradual conceptual development might be an explanation for the students' satisfaction or frustration reported in Martin and Ramsden's study (1985). At the beginning of their first year at university the students in the learning-to-learn programme were frustrated and felt that their needs and expectations were not met, whereas the students in the study skills programme were satisfied and felt that they got out of it what they had hoped for. The reverse pattern was found at the end of the year.

The present study shows that the two types of learning skills programme need not be mutually exclusive or incompatible, but that the positive features of both programmes can be combined in one, and the negative characteristics can be avoided at the same time. For instance, students' initial frustrations can be avoided by meeting their expectations and need for induction, information, guidelines and a certain framework which can easily be provided — for example, in written guidelines and introductory lectures as in the Martin and Ramsden case study or, as Eizenberg (1986) suggests, in the first strategic step of his three-step transition: from 'a more primitive stage of intellectual development' (or the students' initial desire to build up their knowledge as quickly as possible) via a stage of questioning and of an awareness of alternatives, to a stage of review and modification of conceptions by the 'relativistic reasoner'.

In the formal higher education system, there are certain constraints, rules, standards and institutional expectations which students want to know as soon as possible and which they accept in this initial developmental stage when first enrolling in a programme. Once this institutional framework and the points of reference are clear to the students, the learning-to-learn programme can follow and succeed, especially if it is not limited to the first year of study, but conceived as valuable for, and implemented throughout, students' undergraduate and even postgraduate programmes.

Notwithstanding our compromises to institutional constraints, staff attitudes and students' conceptions and needs, our ultimate goal in higher education must be to encourage students to be responsible for, and in control of, their own learning, and to make the conceptual change from learning a science (i.e. a subject or discipline) to becoming a scientist and problem-solver, independent of their teachers' attitudes, beliefs and methodologies. In order to achieve this ultimate goal, initial interventions, such as a learning skills programme, may be designed by progressive teachers and educational advisers. Other teachers in higher education may then gradually be induced to adopt this student-centred and process-oriented approach to higher education, for instance through influence from their colleagues or the students who have become 'personal scientists', or through participating in learning skills workshops.

A brief description of the development of such a learning skills programme integrated into the Foundation Course (i.e. first year of interdisciplinary study) in the School of Modern Asian Studies (MAS) at Griffith University now follows. Examples are presented of the content and functions of workshops and of the introductory lecture, of strategies of helping teachers 'teach' student learning skills, and of strategies of helping students learn. Principles and conclusions derived from this case study may be useful to other HE institutions intending to introduce or revise their learning skills programmes in the light of our experience.

## Integrating learning skills into a first-year programme

Admittedly, in 1979 when we first planned the introduction of a course on 'student study skills' related to and required in the first-year academic programme in MAS, we envisaged the development of basic skills and techniques which we had identified as lacking in many students — high school leavers as well as mature students. One year later, in 1980, it became apparent from discussions in staff meetings that there was a need for developing the higher level cognitive skills defined by Bloom (1956) and for emphasising the process of learning in combination with the content and basic skills of acquiring knowledge of a subject. This focus on the process and content is called *metacognition* or *metalearning*. In subsequent years, the emphasis has shifted more and more from 'student study skills' to a metacognitive approach to 'learning-to-learn' until finally, in late 1985, a review committee of the MAS Foundation Course decided to change the label of 'student study skills' to the more appropriate term 'learning skills'.

*Description and examples*

Table 4 presents an outline of the sessions in the MAS Learning Skills Programme. All learning skills relevant to university study are discussed in workshops throughout the MAS Foundation Course in small groups with teaching staff and work carried out on course materials. Each study task is followed by a reflection on and discussion of the individual students' approach to the particular task. For example, when asked to bring and compare their lecture notes of a specified lecture in the course, students become aware that taking notes is an individual skill which reflects their understanding or misconceptions, dependent on the lecture topic, on the number and type of handouts distributed and on the individual lecturer's style of presentation, and that it is a skill which can be developed. This metacognitive awareness is especially important for students' tutorial tasks — not only for presenting their own papers, but for participating in the discussion of other students' presentations. In one workshop, students in a video-recorded role-play discuss a topic and reflect on the process of this discussion. The topic is designed to be controversial,

**Table 4** *The learning skills programme in the MAS Foundation Course 1986*

1. *Introduction to university study and learning skills.* A lecture providing an overview of the learning skills programme, including information and retrieval, writing, discussion, maths and study skills.
2. *Library skills.* After an introductory lecture on the use of the library and a video programme, students are provided with a technically incomplete list of references, and required to find the call numbers and complete citations of books, articles and primary source materials in the library. In a subsequent session they receive the right answers on a handout and discuss any problems they might have encountered.
3. *Essay writing skills.* After viewing a film on the problem of world poverty and overpopulation, students discuss possible solutions to this problem with staff in small groups. Students are then required to write a 'diagnostic essay' which is marked, corrected and commented on by MAS staff, but not weighted for assessment. The main purpose of this exercise is to identify those students who need immediate help in academic writing (e.g. in basic English grammar, structure, style, punctuation, etc.), which is provided by a specially appointed essay counsellor; and to give students initial practice in, and feedback on, their essay writing within the parameters of this course, but without stress or anxiety. After a session on 'Citations and Bibliographies' and a session on 'Punctuation and Grammar', which are followed by a 'Writing Review Quiz', all essays in MAS must conform to accepted academic standards for format, use of citations, and presentation of bibliographies. If these technical aspects are deficient in an essay, it will be returned with the mark of R, equal to 'Resubmit'. Once accepted for marking, an essay is primarily assessed for its content and the quality of its argument(s). Essays subsequent to the 'diagnostic essay' have increasing difficulty, length and bibliographic requirements, and are returned by teaching staff with written comments and oral explanations when requested.
4. *Discussion skills.* Students learn about group dynamics and effectiveness through a role-play discussion, video self-confrontation and analysis. In two sessions students work out:
   - what the supportive and disruptive elements to effective discussion are;
   - how they can ensure that tutorials provide optimal learning opportunities for all students; and
   - the role of the tutor and the group members.

   In two further sessions students discuss the objectives and tasks of tutorial presentations, responses and group discussions.
5. *Maths skills.* Within the course block on 'Quantitative Methods in the Social/Historical Sciences', there is a 'Maths Review Session' that covers basic numeracy skills and is followed a week later by a 'Maths Review Quiz'

**Table 4 continued**

which is marked but unweighted. Students who have difficulty with the quiz are encouraged to attend additional 'Maths Review Sessions' in subsequent weeks and to take subsequent versions of the quiz until they can pass it.

6. *Study skills.* These workshops aim to raise students' awareness of personal differences in approaches to study, of academic requirements and how to best meet them. Examples include reading for tutorials; time management; taking notes from lectures, books and articles; preparing for and sitting examinations.

---

but related to the course: 'Australia's future lies in its forging closer relations with Asia and reducing its historical ties with the West'. In a second workshop the video recording is played back (in parts) and analysed. The aims of these workshops are:

1. to give students some idea of how small groups work — or do not work — and of the steps we can take to ensure that they operate with the maximum efficiency; and
2. to develop in students, by reflection on the roles they and others play, an understanding of group dynamics, of elements which obstruct an effective discussion, and of group maintenance tasks, together with an awareness of what are supportive and disruptive elements.

This awareness and recognition of discussion dynamics and skills are supported by video self-confrontation and video analysis. It is interesting to note that some students reported that they kept reminding each other of certain roles, functions and behaviours later on in the year whenever tutorials tended to be dominated or disrupted by individuals. ('Remember week one!' emerged as a kind but effective signal.)

The idea of these learning skills workshops in the Foundation Course is to set the scene and to assist a process of students' metacognitive awareness, of learning-to-learn and of their taking responsibility for their own learning, individually and as a group. The teaching team can then provide support, guidance and resources in the actual development of student learning throughout the course.

In the first four weeks there are 15 learning skills sessions. At the end of the first term there is a workshop on examination skills, designed to reduce anxieties by familiarising students with the format, types and content of the exam questions and by giving them practical exercises. These are usually essay-type questions from previous examinations which students answer under exam conditions and evaluate immediately with their lecturer leading the workshop. At the beginning of the second term there are three workshops in which students review the learning skills they have developed so far: a 'Review of the End of Semester I Examination', a 'Review of Essay Expectations' and a 'Review of Tutorial Performances'.

The last four weeks of the MAS Foundation Course include problem-solving — which is the highest cognitive skill and includes problems analysis, synthesis of solution, creative 'brainstorming' and evaluation. Students are allocated to research groups of about 30 members each, working as a team on an interdisciplinary problem in Australian–Asian relations. The objectives of these problem-solving workshops are:

-   to increase students' abilities to analyse complex problems by breaking them down into smaller and more 'workable' components so as to facilitate individual research on these sub-problems and then to assemble the results of this questioning and research into an overall 'solution';
-   to increase students' appreciation of the problems and benefits of functioning as members of a problem-solving group;
-   to help students develop an ability to define and defend their own ideas and the results of their research, and to criticise constructively their colleagues' ideas and findings in an open-ended forum situation where there is not necessarily a 'right answer';
-   to help students develop their knowledge of Asia as a whole rather than as a series of compartmentalised blocks;
-   to stimulate an appreciation and understanding of the ways in which the concepts, techniques and results of the various social sciences which have been introduced so far can be applied to the analysis of complex problems.

Moss and McMillen (1980) describe the teaching strategy of this major problem-solving exercise, they identify and discuss important issues in the process and they evaluate students' experiences and the educational value of these workshops for first-year students.

When revising the learning skills component in 1983 it became clear from students' suggestions and criticisms (in a questionnaire survey) that they needed some information, guidelines and an overview of the whole learning skills programme in order to understand the objectives of each skills workshop, how the skills were related to their programme of study and how they were interrelated.

*Introductory lecture*

Since then, in Orientation Week every year, a lecture entitled 'Introduction to University Study and Learning Skills' explains the rationale for integrating learning skills into the first-year academic programme; it explains the difference between study at high school and at university, and between a 'surface' approach to study and a 'deep meaning' approach to study (i.e. memorising, learning by rote, reproducing knowledge versus trying to understand the meaning to link new ideas and concepts to one's existing knowledge and personal experience).

It is pointed out to students that one of the main goals of higher education is to develop a critical mind, rather than to accumulate a vast amount of factual knowledge. Rather than memorising facts, students should try to look for key concepts or ideas and learn the methods of how and where to find the facts. They should be able to retrieve information and to transfer and apply it to new fields and tasks,  to relate it to their personal knowledge and experience. They should try to understand, to reflect, to analyse, to interpret, to discover and eventually to create new knowledge.

It is further pointed out to students that this process of learning obviously takes longer than rote learning, but that it has a long-term effect: the learning retention rate is higher. Therefore, students should not accept the authority of a lecture or book passively and uncritically, but learn to listen and read critically and actively 'beyond the information given' (Bruner, 1975). The teaching team tries to assist students in this active process of concept learning, meaningful learning, and learning by discovery through appropriate learning-teaching strategies. We refer to educational research which has established that the traditional lecture is an appropriate method to teach factual knowledge, but that creative, critical thinking and analytical skills are more effectively developed through discussion or exercises, workshops, problem-solving and experience-based learning activities (Bligh, 1972).

It could be argued that the expository approach of the introductory lecture is inappropriate for the topic dealing with developing students' study and learning skills through active participation in small-group discussions and workshops. We have therefore included a group dynamic 'listening exercise' at this point in the lecture to provide students with a forceful experience whereby they realise that it is possible to avoid active participation and interaction in a lecture or in an anonymous large group, but not in a one-to-one or small group situation. They also come to realise that this is the reason why we have introduced workshops (rather than lectures) in which students can actively discuss and develop their skills. The remainder of the introductory lecture is devoted to an overview of the purpose, activities, structure and learning-teaching strategies of each workshop. The latter are similar in structure to those suggested by Gibbs (1981).

This introduction to study in higher education also aims to make students aware of the role of a teacher in higher education, a role which is changing from lecturer to facilitator or manager of learning; and it aims to help students understand why they will be given questions to answer in tutorials and essays, and problems to solve in workshops and in individual or group projects, instead of being provided with the answers by staff in lectures. However, these aims cannot always be achieved, because of staff attitudes and beliefs as discussed below.

## Helping teachers learn

Problems sometimes arise in this programme because it is taught by about 15 members of staff from various disciplines and areas of study, some of whom do not agree with the philosophy of Griffith University and its emphasis on small-group work, problem orientation, team teaching and an interdisciplinary approach. It is obvious that students will not adopt certain orientations unless they are encouraged and modelled by the teaching staff. Even though academics may publicly commit themselves to the progressive ideas discussed above, in actual practice they often retreat to a traditional approach which in turn makes students adopt that approach. This phenomenon is explained by Argyris (1980), who distinguishes between 'espoused theory' consisting of our publicly proclaimed values, and 'theory-in-use', consisting of 'governing values' and unconscious strategies over which we have little or no control. Fleming and Rutherford (1984) have applied this theory to academic staff. Entwistle (1984), too, points out that lecturers' educational objectives in higher education are frequently inconsistent with their teaching practice. There is a lack of relationship between intention (what lecturers say they want to do) and performance (what they actually do), between the formal and the 'hidden' curriculum. The former demands:

> originality, problem-solving, independent thought, and analytical skills. In contrast, the hidden curriculum — the message received implicitly but strongly by students — depend[s] on the teaching methods and assessment procedures, and these encourage ... question-spotting and rote memorization of facts and theories considered important by the teachers (Entwistle, 1984, 4).

Other academics have openly admitted that they reject the goals and objectives of the formal curriculum at Griffith University; they adhere to a traditional paradigm of learning, teaching and research. We tried to overcome the problem of staff inertia or inexperience in appropriate teaching methods by three strategies. Initially, we held a workshop on conducting small-group sessions for all staff teaching in the Foundation Course. Full attendance was the result of the school Dean's support and his strong letter of invitation. Although this workshop in early 1981 (before teaching started) was successful in the sense that feedback from participants was very positive, as a single event it was insufficient for staff to learn how to conduct learning skills workshops. More time should have been devoted to this new task which is unfamiliar and hence difficult for academics. In one instance, a lecturer consulted the manual containing the suggested programme aims, content, structure, procedure, etc.) five minutes before the start of his workshop. His students found this particular workshop confusing and a waste of time. In informal discussions with staff I noticed that other colleagues, too, assumed that, compared with a lecture, they need not spend as much time on preparing for a workshop.

Lack of staff training in the workshop method might constitute one of the biggest problems in introducing and integrating student learning skills workshops into academic programmes. Apart from conducting the staff workshop mentioned above (which was only a start and should have been repeated several times, as staff themselves have pointed out), we tried to overcome the staff training problem by two further strategies. We took the easiest way out by selecting those university teachers for conducting the learning skills workshops who were keen, committed to the idea of 'helping students learn' and best able to facilitate student learning through the effective use of the workshop method. This might have contributed to the positive outcome of three surveys of student opinions of the learning skills component throughout the course in 1981. However, selecting staff for teaching skills defeats an important purpose and principle: namely that all faculty staff should teach skills as well as academic content in an integrated way, for they are in the best position to introduce, follow up and further develop learning skills and methods throughout the course. This at least should be our ultimate goal.

Our third strategy to overcome the staff-training problem and to prepare academics for their role as facilitators and managers of learning was the introduction of an Excellence in University Teaching (EUT) programme for MAS staff as a trial in 1985. Although participants evaluated this programme (in open-ended questionnaires and audio-recorded interviews) as being successful, the problem with EUT is similar to problems with other staff development activities: the best teachers attend; those who need to develop skills have excuses for not attending.

But like students who do attend the lectures and tutorials which are the most interesting, instructive and stimulating, academics, too, are likely to participate in staff development if they experience (or perceive by word of mouth) a direct relevance and benefit to their professional lives and careers. We were surprised to hear that some participants in the evaluative discussion after the EUT programme expressed their intention to take part again in the next year's revised EUT programme. Originally we had designed the programme for staff as a one-off series of workshops. Then we realised that it should be an ongoing occasion for helping staff develop and refine the individual and collective skills of facilitating student learning.

**Helping students learn**

How can teachers in higher education best help their students learn? Before embarking on the design of a programme as a solution to these student problems, the Centre for the Advancement of Learning and Teaching (CALT) wrote to all universities and other major HE institutions in Australia and New Zealand in 1979 to enquire about their strategies of helping students learn. We were surprised to find from their responses how little systematic and integrated work had been done in this area. Apart from the traditional student counselling services, there were the odd voluntary, general (i.e. subject-unrelated) workshops and many handouts or booklets on the various study skills. We selected the best handouts for our students, obtained copyright and compiled them in a short version of 'Student Learning Skills Guidelines' distributed free of charge to all first-year MAS students for constant reference and, before each workshop, for reading the relevant chapter. CALT in consultation with MAS teaching staff then designed the student learning skills component integrated into the Foundation Course, using course material as described above and summarised in Table 4. By 1980, the features of our approach were:

1. the integration of course content and learning discussions or metalearning. (Students reflected on the processes of learning and studying immediately after or while doing tasks in the coursework);
2. teaching staff (rather than educationalists or student counsellors) as workshop leaders and facilitators of learning;
3. the administrative integration of the learning skills programme into the normal timetable of the course.

Meanwhile, other institutions have used similar integration models.

In the first year of introducing the learning skills component in the MAS Foundation Course, CALT staff conducted the workshops for one group of students; these were also attended by MAS teaching staff who then conducted the same workshops with their groups of students. In the following year, a manual was produced with the aim of assisting faculty staff to conduct student learning skills workshops independently (and without CALT modelling). Feedback from staff and students suggests that there are academics who are excellent workshop leaders and who would no longer need any assistance from CALT, and that there are others whose workshops (and tutorials) are boring because their sessions consist more of lecturing than student discussion. It is interesting to note that the former group of staff continues to seek a dialogue and collaboration with CALT staff to further improve student learning conditions, but that the latter group does not. It is also interesting to observe that this innovation (of helping students learn) as well as other progressive approaches (e.g. systematic evaluation of teaching for summative purposes; evaluation of courses for formative purposes; review of whole programmes, etc.) in MAS have created a more open and critical learning-teaching environment in which student criticism is not only accepted, but encouraged by more and more staff.

It is increasingly difficult for staff who adhere to a traditional paradigm of higher education not to be affected directly or indirectly by the pressure from students and peers to become more student-centred and process-oriented instead of merely lecturer-centred and content-oriented. However, this change is slow. Yet there is enough reason to proceed with strategies such as the EUT programme and to provide a forum for staff to discuss problems of learning and teaching and ways in which we may help students learn more effectively. For example, in late 1985, a review committee of the MAS Foundation Course decided:

1.  to call a meeting of all staff involved in conducting the learning skills programme in 1986 in order to discuss its aims and conduct; and
2.  to plan two workshops (before the first term in 1986) for all 15 academics teaching in the Foundation Course in order to discuss and standardise the conduct of tutorials and the assessment of oral presentations, as well as essay marking (criteria and aids for students to improve their writing).

For, as other studies have shown (e.g. Ramsden, 1984; Ramsden and Entwistle, 1981), the success of a learning skills programme (in terms of student achievement and approaches to study) largely depends on the educational context. Whether the majority of students adopt a deep or surface approach to learning mainly depends on their perceptions of their teachers' expectations and of assessment requirements. Thus we hope to ensure optimal learning conditions for our students by

1.  selecting and training the very best teachers to conduct learning skills workshops; and

2. involving as many of the teaching team as possible in discussing and negotiating criteria and procedures for assessment which encourage students to adopt a deep approach to learning and a holistic study orientation rather than a surface approach and an atomistic orientation.

## Principles and conclusion

From our experience of designing, implementing, evaluating and reviewing a student learning skills component in the MAS Foundation Course, the following principles and conclusions may be drawn. Metalearning (i.e. a focus on the process of learning in combination with the content of the course) helps establish a positive learning environment. A learning skills programme fulfils the function of setting up a learning environment which is conducive to effective learning for individual students as well as for groups of students, and in which the responsibility for the effectiveness of learning from discussion in tutorials or other group activities lies with the students, rather than with the teaching team. For example, in the workshops on discussion skills, students learn about group dynamics and effectiveness through a role-play discussion, video self-confrontation and analysis and, in subsequent tutorials, remind each other of the principles established by themselves for effective group learning. In this way, tutorials can function well even if the tutor is inexperienced.

Students can experience in structured workshop discussions with fellow students that there are certain characteristics, problems and solutions which are common in learning and studying, but that learning can also vary from individual to individual, depending on a person's existing knowledge. For meaningful learning to occur, students must fully understand and integrate new knowledge into their existing knowledge networks. Students become more confident and motivated to learn how to learn when they experience, through discussion, that they can gain insight into their own learning, and that they can develop skills and methods which are best suited to their personal cognitive systems in acquiring knowledge or in solving problems.

Although the workshops should be voluntary — just as lectures and tutorials are — they should be scheduled in the normal timetable of the course. In this way, staff and students are led to consider the development of learning skills and critical thinking as skills which we continue to develop and refine in higher education and throughout life, rather than as a remedial activity (i.e. as skills which should have been developed at high school).

Students attend and appreciate skills workshops if the skills are directly related to, and integrated into, their coursework. This means that they are motivated to develop their learning methods and skills when they perceive an actual need and purpose. For example, they need reading, writing and presentation skills for assessable items such as essays, tutorial papers, examinations, etc. Therefore, student learning skills workshops should be an integral part of the academic programme, using course materials rather than general texts or topics unrelated to the course.

It follows that the academics themselves are ideally suited to teach skills integrated into their course content, rather than outside experts such as student counsellors or educational advisers in higher education research and development units or centres for learning and teaching. There are various ways in which staff can learn how to help students learn, for example, through discussion, reflection and training in staff development workshops; in a coherent programme, such as the Excellence in University Teaching Programme; or in a small group or one-to-one work relationship between teaching staff and educational advisers working on an action research project.

As a result, the teaching academics gain a better understanding of the processes of student learning and of how to teach (i.e. how to help students learn). Staff who are not involved in the learning skills programme and who tend to promote rote/surface learning are under pressure from their colleagues to change their teaching and assessment in order to encourage students to adopt a deep-meaning approach, and if they refuse to respond, they are under criticism from their students and receive low ratings in the system of student evaluation of teaching. For example, in formative evaluations of Asian language courses, students have complained about some teachers treating them like parrots; in summative evaluation, student assessment of individual teachers has had an effect on decisions about their tenure or promotion.

Just as teaching staff can help undergraduate students learn to learn, they can help postgraduate students learn to do research.

# Chapter 3

# Helping postgraduate students learn

## Introduction

There is an increasing body of psychological and educational research into student learning at the undergraduate level and a growing literature on strategies for helping students learn and develop their learning skills. At the postgraduate level, higher education research and development are relatively sparse. It is often assumed in postgraduate education that candidates have developed basic research and writing skills at undergraduate level (e.g. in reading, note-taking, essay writing, problem-solving, information and retrieval skills, etc.) and that they will be able to translate and apply these skills to their thesis research and writing. That is probably one reason why little has been done in higher education to help students learn and develop their research and writing skills. Another reason may be found in the traditional single-supervisor model of postgraduate teaching. Whether and how well a student is guided in the research process and helped in developing skills in thesis writing depends solely on the individual supervisor's available time, attitude and ability to teach these skills. Since, clearly, not all supervisors have the time, attitude and ability, many students are unable to meet the institutional goals and expectations with regard to the quality and presentation of the thesis within the specified time limitations.

However, in recent years pressure has increasingly been exerted on higher education institutions by governments and other funding bodies to improve the quality and effectiveness of postgraduate research and to reduce drop-out and late submission rates. In fact, the seriousness of the problem was already evident in a publication by the Economic and Social Research Council (1 November, 1985) of a blacklist of British institutions ineligible for research scholarships, which was reported by Turney (1985)

> This unprecedented move is the final sanction in the council's campaign to force an increase in PhD submission rates, and comes after strong pressure during the summer from the Advisory Board for the Research Councils. Fourteen institutions, including eight universities, whose latest four-year submission rates for social science PhD awards made in 1979 and 1980 are below 10 per cent, will be debarred from receiving ESRC research studentship in 1986 and 1987. Next year the council will raise the cut off to 25 per cent, which on current figures will bring the bar down on a further 20 institutions.

It is, therefore, more and more important for higher education institutions to discover the reasons why students fail to complete their theses on time or at all, and to design and monitor strategies for helping students (and supervisors) overcome these problems.

Rudd (1984; 1985), Moses (1981; 1984) and Powles (1989a; b) have summarised the main problems identified in the literature on postgraduate education. Of these, students in the School of Modern Asian Studies (MAS) at Griffith University experienced the following problems:

- *inadequate supervision* (Rudd, 1975; 1984; Welsh, 1979; Ibrahim et al., 1980; Moses, 1981; 1984; Beard and Heartley, 1984);
- *emotional and psychological problems:* students' social and intellectual isolation, insecurity as to standards, lack of confidence in their ability to complete their dissertations within the specified time limit or at all (Welsh, 1979);
- *lack of understanding and communication* between supervisor and student (Moses, 1981; 1984; SERC, 1983);
- *students' lack of the fundamentals of scholarship* due to a lack of background knowledge, training or experience in research methods (Welsh, 1979; Zuber-Skerritt and Rix, 1986);
- *late completion and high drop-out rates* (SERC, 1983; ESRC, 1984; CVCP, 1988; Elton and Pope, 1987; Barrett and Magin, 1983).

Various strategies have been suggested to improve the single-supervisor model. For example, Moses (1981; 1984) introduced workshops on postgraduate supervision in which supervisors from various departments discussed their role and functions, their expectations of students' performance, standards and written regulations and guidelines on thesis writing. Moses (1985b) also provides a useful guide on supervising postgraduates. The Science and Engineering Research Council (SERC, 1983) has published a pamphlet for the guidance of supervisors, with a 'check list on good supervisory practice'. Similarly, the Economic and Social Research Council (ESRC, 1984) has produced a publication on 'The Preparation and Supervision of Research Theses in the Social Sciences'. Connell (1985) gives useful advice on 'how to supervise a PhD' at each level of the research process. All these examples are attempts to improve students' research skills from the supervisor's perspective and to assist supervisors in their tasks of helping students research, write and complete their theses successfully, and within the specified period of time. There are also useful resources for students, such as the reference books by Madsen (1983), Howard and Sharp (1983), Ballard and Clanchy (1984) and Phillips and Pugh (1987).

The purpose of this chapter is to demonstrate how learning and research problems in postgraduate education can be identified from the students' as well as the supervisors' perspectives, and rectified by applying the same principles of effective learning and teaching as at the undergraduate level: the facilitation of learning by discovery and through discussion, of metacognition (i.e. a focus on the process of research and knowledge production as well as on the content of research), problem-solving, and a 'deep' approach to study and research (i.e. trying to understand the meaning, and linking new ideas and concepts to one's existing knowledge and personal experience, rather than learning by rote and trying to reproduce knowledge).

These aims of developing postgraduate students' research skills and deep approaches to 'learning to do research' have been achieved through action research methodology. This means teaching academics themselves have been encouraged to do action research into their own postgraduate education practice by working with an educational adviser on a particular project, focusing on a problem (or problems) in their own postgraduate courses or programmes. In brief, this action research involves the following steps in each cycle in the spiral of action research (Carr and Kemmis, 1986):

1. analysing the problem;
2. planning appropriate strategies and interventions to rectify the problem;
3. evaluation;
4. reflection on the results;
5. repetition(s) of this cycle; and

6.  making a contribution to higher education in form of a conference paper and/or a journal article.

All case studies discussed in this chapter are action research projects within this definition (Harris and Zuber-Skerritt, 1985; Knight and Zuber-Skerritt, 1986; Zuber-Skerritt and Knight, 1985; 1986; Zuber-Skerritt and Rix, 1986; and Diamond and Zuber-Skerritt, 1986).

The significance of these projects and the novel features of these case studies may be seen in the fact that the practice of learning and teaching has been improved by the academics themselves who have also produced empirical research and developed theory themselves, rather than merely applying theory provided by educational researchers or theorists.

The progressive development and integration of student research skills in postgraduate programmes are discussed below and then briefly illustrated by five different examples from the School of Modern Asian Studies (MAS) at Griffith University:

1.  a programme review identifying student problems;
2.  the workshop model for developing skills in dissertation research and writing;
3.  the focus on two key problem areas in the process of dissertation writing;
4.  a course on 'Problems and Methods in Research' for the beginning researcher as an alternative model and supplement to the single-supervisor model in postgraduate education; and
5.  student metacognition and learning to do research through eliciting some changing personal constructs of research effectiveness.

## Integrating student research skills into postgraduate programmes

The ability to do research in a discipline or into an interdisciplinary problem depends not only on students' inherent intelligence and tacit intellectual abilities, as is commonly assumed, but also on the stage of their development in the particular area of study. There is an emerging body of research on human developmental stages in knowledge acquisition (e.g. from concrete to abstract) and on the difference between expert and novice representational systems of knowledge. Of particular interest here is the McGaw and Lawrence (1984, 4) argument that:

> Experts' mental models contain abstract principles from their particular domain of knowledge while novices' models contain the literal objects and explicit conditions of the problem statement.

Teachers in higher education should not, therefore, assume that students begin with the same models as they themselves do, or as do more advanced students in that field. It is not necessarily a matter of intelligence, but of their stage of development in that particular subject area. This insight is of special relevance to degree programmes that are interdisciplinary and accept a heterogeneous student population with varying degrees of knowledge in the various subject areas pertinent to the focal field of study. If we ignore the fact that individual students are at different stages in different subject areas, we may tend to believe — and lead our students to believe — that their failure (e.g. to understand the content of a course or to produce a thesis within the required time constraints) relates to their lack of intelligence or their inability to learn and perform. Instead, we should create a supportive learning environment and design appropriate interventions in the curriculum, in our teaching and in our assessment in order to help students develop their conceptual abilities and intellectual skills step by step and from one level to the next through practice, experience, discussion and metacognition. Eizenberg (1986) has shown how this can be achieved in Anatomy, for example, with regard to both 'learner' outcomes (e.g. cognitive structure, stage of intellectual development, level of conception of learning, abilities and skills and versatility of styles of learning/thinking/reasoning) and to 'learning' outcomes at the course, subject and specific learning task levels. His three steps of student learning (when they are confronted with new information) and of teaching strategy may be extended to student metacognition as shown in Table 5.

The case studies in this chapter will illustrate how these steps in student learning and metalearning can be facilitated by the progressive development and integration of student research skills in postgraduate programmes. After a programme review in which student needs and problems are identified, the first step to help students satisfy their need for information (and for building an operational framework) as quickly as possible is achieved through workshop discussions of rules, requirements, expectations and standards. The second step is covered by a course on 'Problems and Methods in Research' with the aim being to raise student awareness of problems in the philosophy of science and in the interpretation of 'facts' and data. Finally, the third step, relating to students' metacognition of the research process and of their personal constructs of research, is facilitated by Kelly's (1955) Personal Construct Theory using the repertory grid technique. However, it might be advisable to first provide the reader with some background information pertaining to the case studies.

**Table 5** *Developmental steps of learning, teaching and metalearning*

| Step | Learning | Teaching | Metalearning |
|------|----------|----------|--------------|
| 1. | Comprehend it | Provide simple concepts and rules | Get information about programme aims, requirements, standards, etc. |
| 2. | Knock it | Teach specifics (questioning the rules and concepts) | Become aware of different approaches, learning processes, research methods and epistemologies |
| 3. | Modify it | Review the principles and concepts in depth, i.e. rebuild a new model in a relativistic form | Learn to do research through problem-solving, a dialectic process of analysis and synthesis, and through metacognition of research effectiveness |

## Background to case studies

All five case studies presented in this chapter have evolved from action research by academics (in the School of Modern Asian Studies at Griffith University) into problems of curriculum and student learning. The postgraduate students involved in these studies are Honours and Master-by-Coursework students. The Honours students are either full-time students in their fourth year of study (for one year), directly after completing their Bachelor of Arts degree, or part-time students (for two years) with a BA degree and professional experience before and during their Honours programme. This programme consists of four semester units (SUs) of coursework, including a one SU course on research methodology, and four SUs of dissertation work. The Coursework Master Programme (CMP) in MAS is a part-time programme involving two years of study. Generally the students, some of whom have not undertaken formal study for many years, are professionals in full-time employment. They are from a heterogeneous background in teaching, the public service, the services, commerce and industry. Their ages vary from the early 20s to the late 60s. For most of them, dissertation research and writing (which constitutes about 40 per cent of the CMP) is a completely new task, even though they may be highly qualified in their own professions. It is no wonder, then, that these students' problems are compounded in comparison with full-time PhD or Master-by-Research students, the majority of whom would normally have undergone some research training at the Honours level (i.e. fourth year). Very few CMP students have an Honours degree. Most are admitted with a BA degree and at least two years of professional experience in an area related to this CMP.

Educational research on postgraduate education (see the studies mentioned above) has been limited to, and has hitherto tended towards, a focus on problems experienced by full-time PhD and Master-by-Research students. These problems are not only similar to those of our Coursework Masters and Honours students, but they are accentuated for the latter category of students by the imposition of severe time limitations, by these students' greater inexperience of research, and — for part-time coursework students — by their full-time work commitments. Any of these factors may contribute to the failure of such students to meet the institutional aims and requirements within the prescribed time limits; at the very least, they may contribute to these students' poorer academic performance.

## Programme review identifying students' problems

Harris and Zuber-Skerritt (1985) have identified students' problems through a review of the CMP in MAS, with Harris tracing the origins and development of the CMP by examining all relevant university and school documents (e.g. agenda and minutes of the decision-making committees) and Zuber-Skerritt evaluating the CMP from the student perspective by obtaining feedback from students enrolled in this programme during the 1981–85 period, utilising questionnaire surveys, video-recorded group interviews and informal discussions. It is interesting to note that both researchers independently arrived at the same categories of student problems and areas of concern. Some of the conclusions of this case study are reproduced below.

In tracing the origins and planning stages of the programme, we were able to identify some of the issue areas that emerged in discussions between the programme's planners and various committees within the university's course approval system. Without entering a discussion here of all the considerations that emerged, it is appropriate to suggest that, at various levels of discussion during these early days, problems (e.g. related to the weight of the dissertation, the number of elective courses to be made available and teaching and assessment methods) and doubts (e.g. regarding student skills) all drew a variety of arguments and responses. Modifications were called for, and made at the planning stage. However, not all agreed modifications were implemented by the staff, so some of the more substantive issues reappeared at the review stages — for example, students' insufficient background knowledge and skills and their need for guidance in research methods and dissertation writing.

The questionnaire used in the survey drew strong responses from students and yielded two substantive problem areas. First, the coursework component of the degree programme provided a level of difficulty that compromised the students' chances of success, essentially because of their lack of conceptual and analytical skills. Hence problems concerning the theory and its 'high level of abstraction' were only exacerbated by another range of problems that included inadequate access to library materials, the small number of participants in elective courses and the difficulties presented by heavy workloads, particularly the amount of reading expected. The second area causing concern was dissertation research and writing. Students argued that more time with supervisors would have facilitated early direction and guidance, and helped to overcome problems of intellectual 'isolation' or 'loneliness'.

The School of MAS, within certain structural constraints, tried to rectify most of the problems identified by the university's Education Committee at the planning and approval stages: first informally and in an ad hoc manner (e.g. private sessions with small groups of students, intensive supervision, etc.), then formally and systematically (e.g. procedural changes, workshops, adjusting the aims of the dissertation and two reviews). Throughout this process the teaching team had to work within the severe constraints inherent in the university's policy on the CMP. These were institutional and structural constraints: on the one hand, there was the pressure on the school to mount this CMP; on the other, there were no additional resources provided by the institution. If it had not been for the dedication of the teaching teams and the reviews in 1983 and 1985, the gulf between institutional goals and student needs and abilities would have been much wider.

Other institutions planning to introduce (or review) a CMP for professionals may wish to consider our conclusions derived from this case study, explained in detail in Harris and Zuber-Skerritt (1985):

1. Define the professional competencies/skills of the target student group before defining the goals/aims of the academic programme.
2. Avoid or bridge the gap between the institutional goals and the students' actual skills and needs:
   (a) Identify individual students' needs for remedial help before the commencement of the course and design strategies for providing this help (e.g. a bridging course, reading lists, group meetings).
   (b) Do not assume that graduate professionals know how to write a dissertation, but offer a workshop course on dissertation research and writing (e.g. Zuber-Skerritt and Rix, 1986; Zuber-Skerritt and Knight, 1985; 1986).

3. Monitor the programme when introducing it for the first time and review its progress in subsequent years on a regular basis, asking for feedback from students as well as for an evaluation from colleagues and an educational adviser.

## The workshop model for developing skills in dissertation research and writing

In accordance with the first two conclusions derived from the above case study and supported by educational research into the progressive development of adult learning (see Table 5), we defined the required skills of our CMP students, identified their needs and designed a workshop course on dissertation research and writing (Zuber-Skerritt and Rix, 1986).

Our aims were to develop student research and writing skills in the supportive context of small-group discussion and interaction among students facing common problems as well as among supervisors, and between students and supervisors. An excellent response rate by both students and supervisors (i.e. through positive feedback in an open-ended questionnaire and video-recorded discussion, and through a very high attendance rate) indicated that the intended aims (of developing students' research and writing skills and consequently of raising the completion rate) had been achieved by the following workshop activities and processes:

- establishing a clear framework;
- discussing dissertation standards and staff/student expectations;
- discussing individual dissertation proposals (design and rationale) in small groups with other students and supervisors;
- analytical critique exercise;
- the use of sources;
- analysis of contradicting sources;
- the 'nuts and bolts' of dissertation research and writing (e.g. the structure and timetabling of the dissertation; note-taking; referencing; writing and presenting the dissertation).

It becomes clear from this list that the activities and processes were designed mainly to meet students' informational needs at the beginning of their first major research project and in their initial developmental stage of research (Step 1 in Table 5).

Feedback from these students in an open-ended questionnaire survey reflected their appreciation of this workshop course for its assistance with their dissertation research and writing as well as for their confidence and motivation. Several students mentioned that their motivation was raised by the process of learning through group discussion and interaction in an unthreatening, supportive environment. In particular, students appreciated the clarification of procedures, tasks and methods; organisation and planning; staff concern and support; opportunity to discover mutual problems and to discuss solutions; opportunity to learn from previous dissertations, practical exercises, video, etc. Typical students' verbatim comments illustrating these points are included in Zuber-Skerritt and Rix (1986).

Student and staff criticisms of the workshops referred merely to the timing, lecture room and an exercise in statistical representation, all of which were easily rectified in the revised programme for the next intake of students.

Our limited experience with a statistically non-significant number of students suggests that these workshops did have an effect on students' academic achievement and attrition rates. For example, Zuber-Skerritt and Rix (1986) have shown that there was some discrepancy in due-date submission, quality and presentation of the dissertations between those students who did not have the opportunity of group sessions on dissertation research and writing (1981/82) and those who did (1983/84). Whereas none of the first group submitted their dissertation by or even close to the due date, seven of the twelve students who attended the workshops submitted their dissertations on time, or with short extensions.

Apart from this improvement of learning and teaching through an intervention within the programme (similar to all the other innovations taking place in every institution all over the world and at all times), other colleagues in MAS and elsewhere could learn from this action research project. The following action research activities took place. First, the convener of the programme, in collaboration with an educational adviser, analysed the problems of the students in this CMP in particular, and in the literature on postgraduate education in general. Second, they designed a workshop course, integrated into the timetable, content and structure of the programme and monitored it during its implementation. Third, they evaluated the success and effectiveness of the intervention by questionnaire survey, semi-structured video group interview, informal discussion and an analysis of dissertation results and examiners' reports. Fourth, they discussed and reflected on these results with colleagues and drew conclusions for the next revised workshop course in this CMP and for postgraduate education generally. These conclusions were accepted and disseminated in the form of conference papers in Australia (Tertiary Study Skills Conference, Deakin University, 1984) and in Britain (Annual Conference of the Society for Research into Higher Education,

London, 1984) and as an article in a European journal (*Hochschuldidaktik*).

## Workshops on key problem areas

Zuber-Skerritt and Knight (1985; 1986) have identified two major problem areas in the process of dissertation research and writing and suggested workshop activities which can help the postgraduate student to overcome these problems. These areas are the definition of the research problem and the planning and writing of the first draft. These research and writing skills are to be developed through the practical guidance, group support, discussion and reflection which occur in the workshop context.

The first phase in the research process which is critical to the progress and performance of the beginning researcher involves the definition, construction and articulation of the research problem itself. Two of the four major reasons suggested by SERC as to why postgraduate students do not complete their theses in the allotted time refer to this stage of problem definition:

1. Students make a slow start, particularly in the area of problem formulation and literature survey; and
2. students get distracted from the main focus of the research project, for example, by reading texts unrelated to the topic.

Since we were concerned that our full-time Honours students should complete their dissertations within one year and our part-time Masters students within two years (as well as completing their coursework), we tried to help them at an early stage in the research process to define their problem. Apart from advice from supervisors and written guidelines, we facilitated structured workshop discussion in which students themselves generated general principles and guidelines through a process of collective reflection and a concentration on individual students' research topics. Each student was asked to prepare answers to the following set of questions:

1. What is your central question or problem?
2. Why is this problem important and worthy of study (significance)?
3. How will you go about it (research methods and underlying assumptions)?

During the workshop, students and supervisors (in small groups) persisted in questioning and probing each student in turn in a constructive and supportive way until the student's central research problem was clearly formulated. Our aim was to help students define their problem and research proposal as early as possible to focus their reading and note-taking and to avoid general time-wasting. Feedback from three different intakes of students (obtained through open-ended questionnaires, audio-recorded interviews and video-recorded group discussions) suggested that our goals were achieved. The following students' comments are typical:

> When reading a book I now keep thinking: why am I reading this? How does it relate to my central question?

> I used to take a lot of notes, but now I focus my reading more and end up with fewer note cards, but these notes are right to the point, and I can actually use them for my dissertation ...

In addition, students appreciated the group support and interaction with fellow students and advice and different perspectives from supervisors other than their own. They also felt more confident about overcoming the first major hurdle in the research process: the research proposal.

The second crucial phase in the research process is the transition from analysis to synthesis — that is, from collection and analysis of data to the writing of the first draft. There is a dearth of research and development in this area, but our experience suggests that it can be a daunting, and in some cases insuperable, task for students to commit their research findings to paper. Again, we designed structured workshop discussions, this time with the aim of assisting students to overcome psychological barriers to writing and to learn how to plan for and write a first draft.

Students were asked:

1. to prepare answers to a series of questions (e.g. the difference between the first and final draft; how to avoid plagiarism; how to present ideas/arguments comprehensible to the reader of the dissertation; what style of language is appropriate to use, etc.);
2. to structure their projects by dividing their topic into chapters with descriptive chapter headings; and
3. to prepare a personal timetable for the various stages in the dissertation writing process.

As in the previous workshop, each student's project was discussed in turn in small groups. This time the student had to explain the rationale for his or her chosen dissertation structure. The group also discussed the difference between first and final drafts. Students realised that in their first draft they should focus on clear concepts, ideas and structure, using various techniques, for example, flow-charts, concept mapping and Vee technique as described by Gowin (1981) and Novak and Gowin (1984), whilst in their final presentation they should be concerned with detail, precise language, fine tuning of the argument and style.

Interviews with students immediately after the workshop (tape-recorded and transcribed) indicated that students benefited from this workshop in at least two ways: they realised that their fellow students shared the same fears and difficulties; and they learnt skills and techniques which helped them psychologically and strategically in their dissertation writing. Two typical student comments from these interviews are instructive:

> I think they (the workshops) focused my ideas so I know exactly what I should expect, especially the idea about the first draft. Because I find now that I'm not so worried that I have to produce a masterpiece the first time, I can just write down my ideas and then correct the draft later.

> I think that this idea of mapping out your chapters before actually starting to write has made me a lot more confident... I think it's been a comfort more than anything else.

One supervisor who attended the workshop recognised the importance of using the first draft as a means to streamline and improve supervision:

> If this works, it seems like a more efficient way of doing things: you get that first draft fairly quickly and you can get comments from your supervisor... In this way, the supervisor is going to be commenting on things which can be fixed up fairly readily, rather than having to go right back to the start later on.

To sum up, the workshop approach seems to be an effective medium for helping students to overcome the major problems in dissertation research and writing through supportive and constructive discussions with fellow students and several supervisors, and through the process of collective self-discovery to a much greater extent than is possible in the single-supervisor approach. Practical guidance and psychological support in workshops is of particular value in the two crucial phases of thesis writing: problem definition and writing the first draft. Failure to overcome these problems at an early stage may lead to failure to complete the thesis on time or at all.

## A course on problems and methods in research

In addition to these workshops, Knight and Zuber-Skerritt (1986) suggest that a course on research problems, methods and thesis writing should be integrated into every postgraduate programme at the beginning of students' research training. Apart from developing students' practical research and writing skills in workshops, such a course should aim at introducing students to, and raising their awareness of, the epistemological and philosophical assumptions which underlie the process of knowledge production central to the research project.

A course on 'Problems and Methods in Research' in the MAS Honours programme at Griffith University has been developed and reviewed every year since 1981. The course concentrates on the following philosophical problems for five of its fourteen weeks:

1. the problem of knowledge production (empiricism, rationalism, and the rejection of epistemology by discourse theory);
2. the problem of causation; and
3. the question of objectivity and of values present in documentary evidence and secondary textual interpretations as well as the researcher's own values.

An important feature of this course is that it is organised around group discussion and interaction. Only five hours out of 42 (plus two practical workshops of three hours each) are devoted to lectures. Students are encouraged to discover for themselves that there are no definite answers to any of the problems raised and they are guided to work towards a personal resolution of those problems through group discussion and reflection with fellow students and members of the teaching team. For example, two sessions (of three hours each) are devoted to text reading and analysis of a set of documents on a particular topic. The purpose is to increase student awareness of problems of interpreting evidence and to allow students to discover for themselves the philosophical assumptions which underpin particular lines of interpretation. A thorough monitoring of the course (by class observation, staff interviews and student surveys) in 1984 revealed that these aims had been achieved.

The second part of the course is occupied by a series of student seminars to give each student the opportunity to present and defend a lengthy design and rationale for her/his research project and to receive supportive criticism, advice and questions from fellow students and the teaching team.

It can be seen, therefore, that the course was designed to provide a supportive environment in which free and critical discussion could take place. Like any other course introduced for the first time, this course had its teething problems. The teaching team in collaboration with CALT has constantly reviewed and improved the course until recently when the results of a CALT survey (commissioned by the School's Honours Board) demonstrated that students appreciated not only the content of the course, but the team-teaching, workshop-oriented approach it had adopted. The following student responses to the survey illustrate this positive feedback:

> There were several activities encompassed in the course which I found very beneficial and interesting. These included the text reading sessions in which students were expected to identify biases and subjectivity in various texts. In these, and in fact in all tutorials, discussion and debate were encouraged. These discussions were not just between the teaching team and the students but also within the teaching team. As a student I found the discussions between members of the teaching team most useful because they helped in clarifying one's own position. It was in these situations that I realised how valuable the team-teaching method can be.

> I was impressed with this course for a number of reasons, but chiefly because of the attempt to make students more aware of the relationship between theory and fact in social science research. Content and structure of the course were geared to helping students understand the pitfalls inherent in accepting empirical data as the sole criteria of 'truth'. A great deal of importance was placed on the need to look for the theoretical assumptions underlying all so-called objective facts. I found this approach invaluable.

> The course made me aware of problems in research that I didn't know existed before. Basically, it was one of the most interesting and instructive courses I did in my four years in the School of Modern Asian Studies. It was the most valuable course I did in my Honours year.

It is interesting to note that attendance at the workshops, even though voluntary, has been almost 100 per cent in both the Honours and the Masters programmes. This is in line with the very high attendance rates achieved throughout the course on 'Problems and Methods in Research', and reinforces the views expressed in the survey mentioned above that students have found the course useful and relevant to their own individual research projects.

Each student's project is integrated into the course and all activities in this course are directly relevant to the student's research and dissertation writing, as shown in Figure 4.

To sum up, we suggest that the single-supervisor model should be improved and supplemented by other strategies — by the workshop model or a course on problems and methods in research which would be integrated into a postgraduate programme and which would have the following advantages:

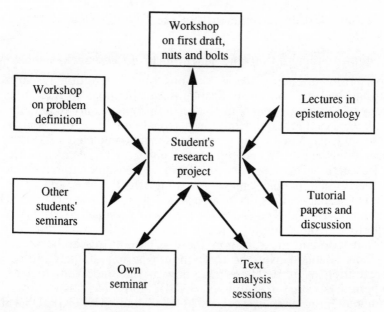

**Figure 4** *The relevance of course activities to the student's research project*

1. Several supervisors could contribute to the course and create a more open and co-operative environment of learning and research. In general, students would learn the foundations of academic research in theory and practice through group discussions with fellow students and several members of staff.
2. In particular, students would be assisted in the crucial problem areas in the research process through mutual support and interaction, that is, in defining their research problem, writing their proposal (design and rationale) and writing the first draft.
3. The course would provide a support system boosting student morale and self-confidence, and lowering attrition and late completion rates.

With reference to Table 5, students in this methodology course become aware of different philosophical assumptions and research methods before making a decision on which approach to take in their own dissertation. They learn to do research through problem-solving and through a dialectic process of analysis and synthesis. This process can be enhanced through students' metacognition of research effectiveness, as the following and final case study shows. For a more detailed

51

discussion of this research project see Diamond and Zuber-Skerritt (1986).

## Student metacognition and learning to do research

Apart from attending the workshops (on dissertation research and writing) and the course on 'Problems and Methods in Research', one group of Honours students in 1985 had the opportunity to participate as volunteers in a research study on personal constructs of research. All eight students in this group responded to and completed a repertory grid form at the beginning and end of the course on 'Problems and Methods in Research'. This repertory grid form was designed to elicit students' formerly tacit perceptions of research effectiveness and to use the computer-analysed results as a basis for 'learning conversations' (Pope and Keen, 1981). Kelly's (1955) theory of personal constructs and its repertory grid technology made it possible for this case study to demonstrate and measure how these beginning researchers' construct systems changed over the three-month period of their professional preparation as researchers, and how it differed from that of four experienced staff researchers. This study has also shown how computer programmes, such as FOCUS and SOCIOGRIDS (Shaw, 1984), can aid students and staff in learning about their own theories of research and in learning from their own experiences of the research training process. It also shown how the use of the computer can promote greater personal control over the construction and negotiation of meaning in postgraduate education, and demonstrated that the repertory grid is a potentially powerful tool which can shed light on people's existing and changing personal constructs. The following are the authors' main conclusions.

By comparing the results of the pre-course with the post-course grids (before and after their methodology course) eight postgraduate students discovered considerable developmental changes in their perceptions of the scope, delineation and clearer definition of what constituted for them good, effective research. Comparison between the students' pre-course mode grids (i.e. group grids) and those of four academic staff (involved in these students' postgraduate training) showed the following results. First, while the students developed clearer ideas of themselves as researchers, these ideas were not realised at the end of the course. Second, the students did not feel that they closed the gap between themselves and their research ideals (i.e. those whom they considered to be good researchers). Third, on each occasion the students felt more like poor researchers than the staff did.

In a final evaluative discussion, both the students and staff confirmed that the grid results validly reflected their emerging or firm views of research and that the aims of this case study had been achieved: to help these students to learn to do research by making their personal constructs of research more explicit and by focusing on the researcher and the research process rather than the final product. In addition, the staff were able to use the students' results for course evaluation and review, and the students' self-confidence was boosted because they discovered that they were incipient 'personal scientists', able to generate their own views and theories, and independent from other researchers' views. This experience of active involvement with their own and others' ideas encourages students to see themselves as more powerful forces in controlling their own learning.

The significance of this study lies in its potential implications for further development and research at other higher education institutions. Two examples may suffice. First, all staff in a department or school involved in postgraduate education could be requested to complete a graded version of our repertory grid form (published in Zuber-Skerritt, 1985) in order to provide a focused snapshot of each supervisor's personal views of research. This could form the basis for his or her discussion with prospective or present postgraduate students. A list could be published of the main personal constructs of research held by staff in that department or school. This information would help students to be guided (as to staff views, methodologies and expectations) from the very beginning rather than only finding out by trial and error or too late; it might also alleviate the problem of students' lack of perception of standards and the problem of a mismatch between the supervisors' own theories and methodologies and those of their students.

Second, postgraduate students could benefit from completing the grid form for several reasons: it would enable them to see their own progress by comparing their grids with those of others or with their own grids completed at different stages in the research training process; and it would help them to articulate 'learning conversations' with themselves, with their supervisors and with fellow students. However, the repertory grid is not a panacea for the problems in postgraduate education, especially when it is not followed by discussion or 'learning conversations', because the construct labels and their meanings would be understood variously by different people. All learning faces this language problem, which can be overcome by discussion of meaning.

### Conclusion

This chapter has attempted to illustrate ways in which to help postgraduate research students learn. The first step should always be to identify students' problems from the students' as well as the staff and institutional perspectives and then to design strategies likely to alleviate these problems. Such strategies might vary from programme to programme and from institution to institution. In the case of the Honours and Master's programmes in the School of Modern Asian Studies at Griffith University, the following methods have proved to be successful within a conceptual framework of higher education that facilitates the satisfaction of students' needs at various developmental stages of their learning (see Table 5):

1. identifying and meeting students' informational, motivational and social needs at the beginning of the programme and providing a supportive environment through workshop discussions;
2. discussing key problem areas in the process of dissertation research and writing, as well as in workshops;
3. raising students' awareness of alternative approaches, epistemologies and research methods in a course on 'Problems and Methods of Research', but again, predominantly through discussion, not through the method of lecturing; and
4. helping students review their personal constructs of research effectiveness through the repertory grid technique and subsequent metacognition or 'learning conversations'.

These learning discussions focused mainly on the processes of research and on changes in the development of individual construct systems as well as in the group modes. Feedback from staff and students suggests that a focus on learning processes as well as content may assist students not only in coping better with their academic tasks, but in being more confident and motivated in their study.

This chapter has also tried to point to action research as one possible method and process to bridge the gap between theory and practice by starting with practical problems of students, staff and curriculum; by reflecting with the people concerned on possible, practical solutions, implementing and evaluating these strategies; reviewing the results; and starting a new cycle of similar activities (of analysing, planning, acting, evaluating, reflecting) in the continuous spiral of action research (Carr and Kemmis, 1986). In the process of this action research, teachers in higher education, themselves actively involved, have gained insights into student learning and generated their own theories and principles, in essence not unlike those produced by educational researchers, but more powerful for having been self-discovered. The teams involved in the studies discussed in this chapter have generated new knowledge about how students can be helped practically to develop their learning/research skills within their academic programmes, knowledge which has been applied in practice to subsequent intakes of students and by new staff in MAS.

Similarly, students have generated knowledge about their own learning and research, about the processes and methods which are best suited for their individual styles of learning, and construct systems, knowledge which they have gained through discussion and self-discovery (rather than lectures and books) and which they will be able to apply to subsequent research tasks in their study.

The limitations of this chapter and the previous one are clear: the proposed integration model of skill development in student learning and research has been successful in the educational context of *one* university, from the perspectives of those involved and with regard to their needs and perceptions. More research needs to be done, for example, to evaluate the effectiveness of these approaches in relation to academic achievement, drop-out rates and late submission and completion dates.

Compared with other studies in the all too scarce literature on postgraduate education, the contribution of the case studies outlined in this chapter (and published elsewhere) is different and new in at least four respects. First, problems have been identified from the student perspective (as well as from the staff and institutional perspectives). Second, some strategies have been suggested towards solving these problems, beyond the advice on supervision given previously (e.g. SERC, 1983; Connell, 1985; Moses, 1985b; Phillips and Pugh, 1987; Elton and Pope, 1989). Third, the focus has been on postgraduate coursework students (in a CMP and in an Honours programme), rather than PhD and Master-by-Research students as in previous research studies. The problems are similar for both coursework students and higher degree-by-research students, but they are accentuated for the former students by their greater inexperience in research and dissertation writing and by the imposition of severe time limitations. Fourth, the emphasis has been on the process of learning/research rather than the outcomes of postgraduate education.

The emphasis on the process of learning and researching for both staff and students is further discussed in the next chapter, which presents a powerful heuristic methodology for eliciting personal constructs of research, teaching and professional development.

# Chapter 4

# Eliciting personal constructs in higher education

## Introduction

For anyone involved in effecting change in people, be they students or staff who want to learn and develop their knowledge and skills, it is important to investigate the current state of the learner and to help him or her to articulate personal theories, to compare them with those of others, to negotiate their meaning and to revise them continually. This chapter explores how this can be achieved most effectively.

Traditional methods, such as the questionnaire and structured interview, have the advantage of allowing data collection from a statistically significant number of subjects, required in large-scale quantitative studies; however, they have the disadvantage of the researcher influencing the subjects' responses by means of questions or non-verbal suggestions. The language and criteria determined by the 'expert' researcher might be alien to the subjects' own personal construct systems and, therefore, be misunderstood by the subjects. Consequently, their responses are likely to be inaccurate or personally invalid. Interview data, whether collected in the form of written notes or transcribed from audio or video recordings, are always the product of an interactive communication. As Pope and Denicolo (1986) argue, the ensuing verbatim transcript is the result of several influencing factors: the interviewer's own personal intuitive theories; the questions

56

in his/her mind which originally defined his/her research; his/her skills in perceptive listening and questioning techniques; and ideas and questions which develop during the interactions with the interviewee. Given these caveats and in order to circumvent them, this chapter argues for the use of a more sensitive instrument, the repertory grid technique, by which people can construe their personal theories of a particular topic without the researcher's influence, but by comparing people or things they know well from their previous experience and by expressing the similarities and differences in abstract terms.

The repertory grid technique has been widely used in psychology and management training, but very little research has been undertaken in higher education except in teacher education. For example, Pope and Keen (1981) have reconceptualised personal construct theory in education in general; Diamond (1983; 1985) has used the repertory grid technique in secondary teacher training; McQualter and Warren (1984) in mathematics teacher education; Kevill et al. (1982) for course evaluation and Kevill and Shaw (1980) for evaluating staff–student interactions and teaching effectiveness.

This chapter aims to show how this methodology can be used in higher education. It is structured in four parts. First, it outlines the theoretical framework of Kellys Personal Construct Theory. Second, it explains the repertory grid technique based on Kelly's theory. Third, it presents some examples of recent case studies in higher education which have applied this methodology; and finally, some conclusions are drawn with suggestions for further research.

## Kelly's theory

Kelly's epistemological position is 'constructive alternativism' which assumes that we are not locked in by predetermined events but have a choice of alternatives; and that our present constructs or interpretations of the universe are subject to revision or replacement. This means that people understand themselves and their environment, and anticipate future events, by constructing tentative models or personal theories and by evaluating these theories against personal criteria as to whether or not the prediction and control of events (based upon the models) have been successful. All theories are hypotheses created by people, which may be valid at any particular time, but may suddenly be invalid in some unforeseeable respect and replaced by a better theory.

On the basis of his epistemology, Kelly (1955; 1963) has developed his theory in terms of a fundamental postulate elaborated by eleven corollaries. The fundamental postulate refers to the basic assumption underlying his theory; the corollaries, some of which are relevant to this chapter, are propositions which amplify his psychology of personal constructs.

Kelly's fundamental postulate reads: 'A person's processes are psychologically channellised by the ways in which he anticipates events' (Kelly, 1963, 46). Kelly believes that science and theory building are not the prerogative of scientists, theorists or researchers, but that every human being is a 'personal scientist' and capable of creating theory at various levels. Personal scientists are engaged in a process of observation, interpretation, prediction and control. They erect for themselves a representational model of the world which guides their behaviour and action. This model is constantly tested, modified or replaced in order to allow better predictions and control in the future. People's behaviour in the present is determined by the way they anticipate events in the future through the use of personal constructs in order to forecast events (theory building) or to evaluate previous forecasts and their validity or efficiency (theory testing). This process of knowledge creation and constant review of one's knowledge is applicable to the researcher, to the learner in the formal education system, as well as to people in everyday life. The only difference is the level of theorisation and abstraction.

Kelly's fundamental postulate and his corollaries give a picture of the person/learner as a 'personal scientist', with a hierarchical construction system (Organisation Corollary) which is personally unique (Individuality Corollary) and which can be explored by him/herself as well as by others (Sociality Corollary). Apart from their individuality, a group of people may be similar in terms of their construction of experience (Commonality Corollary). The development of intelligence or conceptual change depends on the permeability (i.e. the degree of openness for change) of a person's constructs (Modulation Corollary) and on the balance between hierarchical integration and consistency of differing constructs on the one hand and their differentiation and inconsistency (Fragmentation Corollary) on the other. Finally, a person is not pre-determined in her/his thinking, but can choose alternatives (Choice Corollary). Her/his construing is both cognitive and emotional; the personal construct system is a holistic entity. If any part within the system is changed, this change will have implications for other parts of the total system.

Although Kelly's view of a person is a holistic one, including cognitive functions and psychological feelings (e.g. fear, anxiety), as well as early experiences and social conditions, he writes almost exclusively about people as personal scientists and cognitive construers of knowledge about the world. For Kelly, learning is the active, creative, rational, emotional, intentional and pragmatic construction of reality. But he knows that all theories, including his own, are human hypotheses which may fit all requirements at a particular time, but may eventually be found wanting in some unforeseeable respect and, therefore, be replaced by a 'better theory'.

## The repertory grid technique

The repertory grid technique is a powerful heuristic tool which can be used not only for eliciting personal constructs, but also as a basis for 'learning conversations' (Harri-Augstein and Thomas, 1979), formative group discussions, problem-solving, negotiation of meaning and decision-making. It was designed by Kelly (1955) and further developed by Shaw (1980; 1984) and others using computer technology. The repertory grid enables the researcher to elicit from subjects constructs which they customarily use in interpreting and predicting the behaviour of those people whom they know well and who are important in their lives. Another important factor is that this technique facilitates the elicitation of constructs and responses from subjects without influencing them by means of questions, as is the case in interviews or questionnaires, for example. The best definition of a repertory grid is given by Shaw (1984, 14):

> A *repertory grid* is a two-way classification of data in which events are interlaced with abstractions in such a way as to express part of a person's system of cross-references between his *personal observations* or experience of the world (elements), and his *personal classifications* or abstractions of that experience (constructs).

In Kelly's method of eliciting personal constructs the subject nominates a certain number of people in his/her life (elements) and is required to compare them in triads and to say in which way two of the three elements — any two — differ from the third in a contrasting way (e.g. flexible–inflexible, authoritarian–democratic, inviting criticism, being threatened by criticism from others, etc.). The words or phrases resulting from this comparison form the construct pair. Thus both the elements and the constructs are nominated by the subjects themselves.

Meanwhile, many forms of repertory grid technique have been developed, some of which represent a significant departure from Kelly's individuality corollary (i.e. persons differ in their construction of events) in that they give the constructs to, rather than elicit them from, the subjects. This means that the assumption behind the use of provided constructs is that people resemble each other in their construction of events. Another development of Kelly's original grid is to provide the elements, and only one construct, with the intention of comparing individual grids and of arriving at a group (or mode) grid.

The process and procedures of using a repertory grid are described by McQualter (1985). Examples of repertory grid forms (to elicit personal constructs of effective teaching, research and professional development) are available from the author with instructions for completing, rating and interpreting the grid. However, experience has shown that the use of repertory grid technology can best be developed in a workshop situation or by hands-on practice under the guidance of a person experienced in this methodology, rather than by reading instructions.

## Uses in higher education

This section deals with four case studies in higher education which are based on Kelly's theory. However, these are not mere applications of personal construct psychology, but also cases in which the participants have adopted a constructivist theory of their educational practice (Novak, 1988). This statement is illustrated by the following five examples: three case studies of staff and postgraduate students' personal constructs of *research* effectiveness at universities in Australia, Great Britain and Germany and a case study of personal constructs of second-language *teaching*. A fifth case study using repertory grid technology is presented in more detail in Chapter 5.

### Research

In the series of case studies eliciting staff and postgraduate students' personal constructs of research effectiveness, the first study by Diamond and Zuber-Skerritt (1986) was conducted with eight Honours students in the social sciences at an Australian university and four staff members involved in teaching their methodology course and/or supervising their dissertations. This study has already been mentioned in Chapter 3 with regard to developing postgraduate students' metacognition and their research skills.

Comparison between the computer-analysed results of the pre-course grids and those of their post-course grids demonstrated considerable developmental changes in the students' perception of the scope, delineation and clearer definition of what constituted for them good, effective research. For example, it demonstrated and measured both how the construing of this group of students changed over the three month period of their professional preparation as researchers and how it differed from that of four experienced staff researchers. The students gained a better understanding of their own formerly tacit perceptions of research effectiveness as well as those of expert others.

The staff learned to use the repertory grid technique as an aid to course evaluation by asking at the end of the course whether students' expectations of research (as delineated in the pre-course mode grid) had been fulfilled.

The second study was conducted by the author (Zuber-Skerritt, 1987a) with six staff and six postgraduate students (MPhil and PhD), all engaged in some aspect of educational research in a British university. On the one hand, the study demonstrated the use and potential power of the repertory grid for better understanding one's own and others' constructs of research and for more fully appreciating different points of view. On the other hand, it pointed to its potential danger and abuse. For a repertory grid can be used as a basis for sharing and negotiating meaning with others in order to solve a particular problem or to make decisions, or it can be a very private matter and should be treated confidentially. But each participant must decide whether the use should be private or public.

The purpose of the study was to use the repertory grid technology for construing and analysing individual as well as group constructs of research effectiveness in order to be able to suggest ways in which these evolving criteria may be met in postgraduate education within or beyond the traditional single-supervisor model. The repertory grid exercise seemed to be an effective way of achieving this goal. As one academic commented:

> As a staff member involved in drawing students' attention to methodological issues, it was of great interest to see the students' mode grid and to hear them talk about their views. Certainly they seem to have thought about the issues, and their ideas in common currency in the department seem to have permeated through the exercise.

Experienced researchers, too, might benefit from the repertory grid exercise, especially from the subsequent group discussion based on the computer analysed results. As another staff member commented:

> Discussion of the results of the grid might show how two people who name a construct using the same or similar terms might have quite different understandings of what that construct means; similarly, two people who use different terms might discover an underlying similarity. Thus, even if discussion of a grid does not enlarge or clarify one's own ideas very much, it might well help people to better understand one another's ideas, and to more fully appreciate different points of view.

The third study in this series (Zuber-Skerritt, 1988) conducted with five academic staff and seven postgraduate students at a German university, demonstrated how the repertory grid was used to elicit, discuss and negotiate staff and students' individual constructs of research, with the result of a greater group consensus and a clearer picture of their shared criteria of research effectiveness. Many of these criteria cannot be transferred to any other group of researchers, because they vary for each group. But this case study provides an example of the kinds of answer we may expect to the question: What constitutes effective research? And it illustrates the use of a method and procedures by which the answers can be found.

Participants in this study recognised that the repertory grid technique was a catalyst, not a definitive account of people's thinking; that the computer could assist in producing fast, useful data in an analysable, standardised form; but that they themselves had to go beyond verbal labels and figures to explore and negotiate their meaning, theories and views in more detail. It was in this spirit that the repertory grid technique stimulated thinking and debate among all students and staff in this academic unit on the nature and effectiveness of their research.

The significance of the three studies relates to the exploration of both the topic of research effectiveness and the use of the repertory grid technology. Similar studies may be conducted on the same topic in other disciplines using the repertory grid technique with or without the computer analyses.

*Teaching*

Finally, the repertory grid may be used to elicit personal constructs of learning and teaching. For example, in a study (Zuber-Skerritt, 1989) of eight language teachers at an Australian university, as part of a wider study on attrition in second-language learning, it was important to establish what the three Asian language teaching teams considered to be constituents of effective teaching. Their agreement on mutual criteria could be used for the evaluation and self-evaluation of their teaching practice. Although these criteria might not be unusual or totally new to other language teachers, the process of construing a constructivist theory of their educational practice was important and developmental to the participants in this study — individually and as a team.

## Conclusion

The above repertory grid studies suggest that this technique is a powerful heuristic tool in higher education, not only to elicit people's present personal constructs of research and of teaching from the researcher's perspective, but, moreover, to help staff and students to become aware of their own and other people's personal perspectives of professional or academic aspects in higher education, and to use the grid results as a basis for discussion, negotiation of meaning with colleagues and for decision-making. Where comparisons of mutual elements and/or constructs are possible, computer technology can be used for a more sophisticated data analysis (Shaw, 1984). This is helpful for the participants' discussion and possible group consensus, leading to mutual criteria of effectiveness which may be used for the evaluation of practice.

However, the repertory grid technique could not be used as a research method without having the participants discuss, negotiate and confirm the results presented by the researcher. It is mainly an instrument to focus a group discussion on some constructs we may share and agree upon, in this case on constructs of effective research and teaching. So the limitations are that these personal theories are not necessarily generalisable and valid to other staff and students in higher education, although they are of direct, practical importance to the staff and students involved in the particular study. Other researchers and teachers cannot rely on the content of the personal theorising by participants in a case study as 'objective knowledge', but they may use the methodology in order to elicit their own theories in their particular context.

It is hoped that this chapter might stimulate further research and development in higher education. Kelly's theory and the repertory grid technique may be used in other areas of higher education, wherever people's personal perceptions and perspectives differ or need to be more explicit, or agreed upon, for example, with respect to effective team work, committee work, administration, etc. This process could also be used in senior management as well as student learning, individually and/or in groups, for example in the area of effective study methods, such as essay writing, reading and note taking for academic purposes, discussion skills in tutorials, etc.

The next chapter provides a more detailed description and discussion of another area in higher education — professional development — that can be explored by means of the repertory grid technology.

# PART III

# REFLECTIONS ON
# ACTION RESEARCH

# Chapter 5

# Reflections of action researchers

## Introduction

This chapter aims to present the reflections of some of those academics who participated in collaborative action research projects in higher education (described in Chapters 2 and 3) as well as my reflections on my own practice in curriculum and academic staff development. To this end, I have chosen a repertory grid study which I conducted with seven action researchers on their personal constructs of professional development. The results are significant in that they suggest that action research is considered by the action researchers themselves to be the most effective method of professional development.

In order to evaluate the effectiveness of action research for the action researchers themselves and for their professional development, I considered the use of an open-ended questionnaire and in-depth interviews, either by myself or by a more neutral colleague. I rejected both methods mainly for two reasons. First, in these surveys which depend upon verbal responses to structured questions (whether in oral or written form), my bias could have been introduced into the very data I was attempting to study. Second, I had personally worked so closely with the colleagues in this division that their responses might have been too favourable. Therefore, I had to use a more sensitive instrument which would elicit their constructs and personal theories of professional development generally, and of action research in particular, without influencing their thinking and rating in any way. The best instrument for achieving this aim seemed to be Kelly's repertory grid technique.

In the following I shall first describe the plan of this case study and the choice of the repertory grid form and of the computer programmes used; then I shall discuss the conduct of the study, including the method, the analysis of the individual grids and of the group (mode) grid; finally, I shall discuss the grid results and the participants' reflections on action research as professional development in higher education.

## Plan

There were several grids and computer programmes I could have used. The ideal technique seemed to be Shaw's PEGASUS, a computer programme in which staff would not only have elicited their own constructs, but would also have chosen their own elements (i.e. the methods of staff development, apart from action research). However, this would have had the disadvantage that the individual grids could not have been compared and no group results would have evolved. Therefore, I had to compromise and design a grid form which provided the elements, but not the constructs, except one supplied construct pair: *Effective–Ineffective*. I had to choose elements which were commonly known, that is, those methods of professional development which academics had experienced in this division. I also had to provide a defining description of the elements in order to avoid confusion as much as possible. These descriptions are presented in Table 6.

The six elements (E1–E6) of professional development known to all participants were: 'Action research', 'Trial and error', 'Reading', 'Observation', 'Formal sessions', and 'Top-down advice'. Figure 5 is the repertory grid form used.

## Conduct

The study was conducted with seven participants, all of whom had had some experience with action research (into developing students' learning and research skills, as described in Chapters 2 and 3) and with subsequent report or paper writing. Their observation of this experience made it possible for the participants to carry out the action of completing the grid form by comparing and reflecting individually on the various methods of professional development they personally knew, thus arriving at abstract conceptualisations of this experience. This reflection phase was then extended by the participants' group discussion based on the computer results.

**Table 6** *Definition of elements in the repertory grid on professional development*

---

E1 *Action research* is defined as the total process of professional development (PD) which finally results in your co-authored report(s), conference paper(s) or journal article(s). This means your own and collaborative activities go through the following cycle:

1. identification of a problem in the curriculum of learning and teaching which you are concerned about;
2. analysis of the problem;
3. decisions about selecting strategies, trying out innovations and devising methods which would solve them;
4. implementation or conduct of the experiment or enquiry;
5. testing and evaluating the innovation;
6. reflection on the results of the evaluation;
7. conclusions and/or identification of a new problem or problems and continuing with a new cycle of this action research.

E2 *Trial and error* (or learning on the job or practice without formal professional development) means 'doing' and acting without direction or guidance — in other words, learning to swim by being thrown in at the deep end. You may remember the situation when you first joined an institution of higher education and, without any sustained professional training, you were required to give lectures, tutorials, workshops; to assess students' work; to design courses, etc.

E3 *Reading* refers to reading papers, books or articles in higher education on any aspect of learning and teaching and of staff development.

E4 *Observation* means observing lectures, tutorials or other aspects of teaching conducted by your colleagues.

E5 *Formal sessions* may consist of staff development workshops or lectures related to teaching, or any other sessions you might have attended in order to improve your teaching. These sessions are normally designed by someone else (e.g. CALT) on topics of general interest to academics (e.g. on lecturing, small-group teaching, assessment, etc.)

E6 *Top-down advice* based on student evaluation of teaching means strong suggestion and direction from the central administration or the Dean or Head for you to engage in professional development. If you have never experienced such advice (as I assume), please try to imagine it, as it presents one possible method of encouraging academics to improve their teaching, especially when there have been student complaints about teaching.

---

REPERTORY GRID FORM:
CONSTRUCTS OF PROFESSIONAL DEVELOPMENT (PD)
OF UNIVERSITY TEACHERS

Name:
Date:

| | *Emergent constructs* | Elements | | | | | | *Implicit constructs* |
|---|---|---|---|---|---|---|---|---|
| | | E1 | E2 | E3 | E4 | E5 | E6 | |
| 1. | | 0 | 0 | 0 | | | | |
| 2. | | | | | 0 | 0 | 0 | |
| 3. | | 0 | | 0 | | 0 | | |
| 4. | | | 0 | | 0 | | 0 | |
| 5. | | 0 | 0 | | 0 | | | |
| 6. | | | | 0 | | 0 | 0 | |
| 7. | | | 0 | 0 | | 0 | | |
| 8. | | 0 | | | 0 | | 0 | |
| 9. | Effective | | | | | | | Ineffective |

E1 Action research
E2 Trial and error
E3 Reading
E4 Observation
E5 Formal sessions
E6 Top-down advice

**Figure 5** *The repertory grid on professional development*

*Method*

Three of the participants knew how to complete the form from their experience in a previous repertory grid study. I introduced the other participants to the method in individual sessions. They learnt to elicit their constructs by comparing three elements at a time — for example, 'Action research', 'Trial and error' and 'Reading' — and to express in a word or short phrase the way in which two of them were similar (emergent construct) and different from the third (implicit construct). For example, *Process of Learning by Experience* was an emergent construct relating to 'Action research' and 'Trial and error'; and *Passive Process of Learning* was an implicit construct relating to 'Reading'. The participants were asked to cross the circles of the two similar elements for each construct and then to rate each element on each construct on a five-point scale, allocating a rating of 1 or 2 to the similar pair and 4 or 5 to the singleton. A rating of 3 meant a medium rating or 'not applicable'. At the end they were asked to rate each element as to its effectiveness (1 or 2) or ineffectiveness (4 or 5) with regard to professional development.

Although the grid may be analysed manually, I decided to use the faster and more sophisticated analysis by Shaw's (1984) computer programmes FOCUS and SOCIONETS as a basis for subsequent 'learning conversations' with the participants.

FOCUS rearranges the columns of elements and the rows of constructs in such a way that there is least difference between the numbers in any two adjacent columns down or rows across the grid. For example, the similarity or percentages of match of adjacent elements and constructs are shown in the element and construct 'trees' in Figure 6. It is important to stress that similarity refers to the way in which the constructs order the elements, rather than by the verbal labels of the constructs. FOCUS thus points to those clusters of constructs and clusters of elements which are most or least similar in the participant's mind.

SOCIONETS is a programme which enables us to analyse a group of grids, if the elements are shared by all participants, as in this case. Mode grids are focused group grids which consist of the most highly matched, and hence dominant, group constructs.

*Analysis of individual grids*

The participants received their individual focused grids with the computer-generated statistical analysis, but they had to add their own personal meaning and confirm or interpret these computer results directly in terms of the original data. It is interesting that all but one action researcher ranked 'Action research' as the most effective

71

approach to staff development. On a five-point rating scale (1 being most effective and 5 least effective), five academics gave 'Action research' a rating of 1; one gave a rating of 2, but rated the other methods lower; and one participant allocated a rating of 2 to 'Action research' and rated 'Observation' higher. Table 7 presents each staff member's effectiveness ratings and the group's average ratings of the various methods of professional development.

## *Analysis of the mode grid*

The participants also received a computer printout of SOCIOGRIDS and of the focused mode grid. Of particular interest is the list of those constructs with the highest average match with all other constructs elicited by the group or, in other words, the dominant constructs of professional development held by this group of academics.

The element tree in Figure 6 shows that this group of academics perceived the following modes of staff development as similar. 'Reading' and 'Observation' are matched at 81 per cent, 'Action research' and 'Trial and error' at 78 per cent, and all four at 75 per cent, whereas 'Formal sessions' and 'Top-down advice' are not seen to be closely matched at all (66 per cent and 61 per cent respectively). It should be pointed out that these similarities do not coincide with the participants' views of effectiveness. For example, 'Action research' and 'Trial and error' were perceived as being similar in some respects (measured against the mode constructs), yet when judged on the criterion of effectiveness, they were at opposite ends (i.e. ratings of 1.3 and 3.9 respectively).

The construct tree (in Figure 6) shows three main clusters of constructs which are matched at more than 80 per cent each and at about 75 per cent altogether. These clusters are:

**Constructs 2, 6, 9, and 11**: *No outside control*; *Not intimidatory*; *Effective*; and *Staff member trying to learn*, rather than merely receiving advice and being subject to outside control or even intimidation. This staff autonomy, self-determination and control over their own professional development are reflected in the next cluster of group constructs.

**Constructs 1, 4, 7, and 15**: *Staff involved in gathering information* (instead of receiving advice without a basis to assess the relevance of it); *Personally initiated* (rather than organised by others and not meeting one's own immediate, practical needs); *Directly involved in the teaching process* (again instead of receiving information from others); and *Opportunity to decide what*

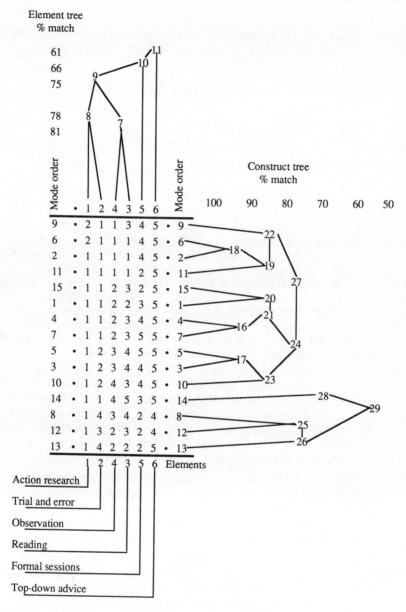

**Figure 6** *Focused mode grid on professional development*

**Table 7** *Effectiveness ratings of various methods of professional development*

| Staff | Action research | Trial and error | Reading | Obser-vation | Formal sessions | Top-down advice |
|---|---|---|---|---|---|---|
| 1 | 1 | 3 | 3 | 2 | 2 | 4 |
| 2 | 2 | 5 | 2 | 1 | 5 | 3 |
| 3 | 1 | 2 | 4 | 2 | 3 | 5 |
| 4 | 1 | 5 | 3 | 4 | 2 | 5 |
| 5 | 1 | 4 | 2 | 2 | 1 | 3 |
| 6 | 2 | 3 | 5 | 4 | 3 | 3 |
| 7 | 1 | 5 | 3 | 3 | 2 | 4 |
| Average | 1.3 | 3.9 | 3.1 | 2.6 | 2.6 | 3.9 |

This table shows that, on average, this group of academics rated 'Action research' as by far the most effective method of professional development (a rating of 1.3) and 'Trial and error' and 'Top-down advice' as the least effective (a rating of 3.9). The relatively favourable view of 'Formal sessions' might be due to the fact that these have been rarely offered at this university, but are seen as desirable, especially after a successful 'Excellence in University Teaching' (EUT) programme which did not consist of top-down expert advice, but of experiential learning in areas directly related to the individual staff members' practice and concerns (Adie et al., 1986). It is interesting to note that staff member 3, who gave a rating of 5, had not attended the EUT programme.

*one needs/wants* (rather than waiting for others to nominate an area of concern). This strong resistance to outside determination of their needs may be seen as closely linked to staff aspiration for development through action as consciously controlled action (Leontiev, 1977) and as practical experience (Kolb, 1984), as emphasised in the next cluster of group constructs.

**Constructs 3, 5 and 10**: *Process of learning by experience* (rather than a passive process of learning and development); *Active, consciously initiated* (rather than passive and not self-initiated); and *Consciously thought out and acted on, on the basis of one's needs*.

As mentioned before, these three clusters of group constructs are matched at 75 per cent. They are also matched at 70 per cent with a single construct, namely 14: *Being active, productive and creative in practice* (rather than being passive and reproductive).

There is a fourth cluster of group constructs which is matched at 75 per cent, but more isolated from the other three clusters and from construct 14 (40 per cent match). This cluster consists of mode constructs 8, 12 and 13: *Utility as a path to problem-solving*; *Effective*; and *Thinking and learning about teaching* (instead of acting on impulse).

From these results it would appear that this group of academics who have experienced the various methods of professional development, including action research, believe that the best way to learn about teaching in higher education is not to be given information and advice (on how to improve teaching) by outside experts who determine what academics need to know. Rather, their theory of professional development is that academics can and should try to learn about teaching as they do in their research about their discipline or particular subject area, that is, as personal scientists (Kelly, 1955) and problem-solvers (Popper, 1959; 1969), through active involvement, practical experience and reflection (or thinking) about this experience (Lewin, 1952; Kolb, 1984; Carr and Kemmis, 1986).

An important condition is that these developmental activities be personally initiated, self-directed and consciously controlled by the academics themselves (Leontiev, 1977). This kind of professional self-development is directly relevant to the teachers' needs; and, as one academic put it, it is active, productive and creative in practice.

However, it is interesting to establish how the academics themselves interpret the results and the implications of the results for themselves, both personally and for their division, institution or the wider academic community.

## Discussion and interpretation of results

This section is an account of the participants' discussion of, and their reactions to, the above analysis of the repertory grids. Verbatim comments from the tape-recorded discussion are presented in inverted commas or as indented quotations.

Five main issues arise from the discussion. First, the participants confirm the results which in turn confirm my own theory of professional development (Zuber-Skerritt, 1992). Second, the element of falsification is introduced by highlighting the participants' concerns about actual professional development in their institution and elsewhere. Third, implications for student learning derived from the discussion are summarised. Fourth, the notion and problem of change is raised from the participants' perspectives. Fifth, the limitations of this study, again as seen by the participants, are presented.

## Participant confirmation

Three of the seven participants in this study were unable to attend the meeting at which my analysis and the results were presented and discussed. This was because they had left the university to advance their careers elsewhere. However, one of the absentees sent us his detailed written comments which were discussed at the meeting; and a visiting scholar (who is an action researcher into teacher education, firmly based on Kelly's personal construct theory, and an expert in repertory grid technology) joined us in the discussion.

On the whole, the above analysis was confirmed by this group of academics in terms of content and method for both the individual grids and the mode grid. The results were then interpreted. For example, the mode element tree was interpreted as follows. 'Action research' and 'Trial and error' were closely matched because both of these methods of professional development were seen as allowing a great deal of freedom, self-initiative and creativity. 'Reading' and 'Observation' were closely matched because they were similarly regarded as activities which could be either passive or active, whilst the more isolated 'Formal sessions' and 'Top-down advice' were matched because they were seen as receptive and passive methods by which to develop staff. However, the latter match was not close (66 per cent), perhaps because these elements were interpreted somewhat differently.

The differences in individual meanings displayed by the repertory grid technique then provided the agenda for discussion. For example, 'Top-down advice' was understood by some participants to mean advice operating as encouragement in the form of supportive guidance, but others saw it as synonymous with compulsion, direction and heavy-handed guidance. This difference in meaning was negotiated in the discussion. However, one academic suggested that, when publishing these results and drawing conclusions from them for what may constitute effective professional development, not only at this university but also elsewhere in higher education, it should be made explicit that the notion and definition of each method of professional development can vary from person to person. This accords with the fundamental postulate of personal construct theory.

## The reality of professional development

Although this group of academics seemed to agree on the nature of and the criteria for effective professional development, they clearly saw that this view was not shared by everyone else in their division. For example, on the one hand, they had agreed that top-down advice, direction and prescription on how to improve teaching were not effective modes of professional development, while on the other hand, they also realised that their ideal of self-direction, self-motivation and action research into learning–teaching problems might not be effective in reality since there are academics who resist new ideas, change and continuous development. One participant succinctly summed up the problem: 'The very people who need to be converted are the people who are most resistant to it. And the very ones who don't need to be converted are the ones who are most open to it.'

The group agreed that those who attended the Excellence in University Teaching programme and those who have participated in action research projects and in this study are the very ones who are motivated and interested in improving their teaching; but the problem identified by this group concerns how to get others to look at their own practice. The following solution was suggested by one participant and found resonance with the group:

> It seems to me that you have to create an environment in which teaching is regarded as a valued activity; it is not just an 'airy fairy' thing; it is related to people's life chances. Therefore, if you are a good teacher, your chance of getting a promotion will be improved. Within this organisation in which we work there is a general philosophy which really highly regards teaching; a lot of thought is given to it; and we talk about it a lot; we are paying attention to what students are saying, and so on. And in that sort of general environment, and especially if there are supportive, encouraging vibrations from the Dean and from the people who are in the positions of authority, then it will be a lot more effective.

Effective teaching and professional development clearly have important implications for effective student learning.

## Implications for student learning

The participants in this discussion considered student learning and professional development as similar processes. Just as in staff learning and development, they believed there also needs to be a balance in student learning between top-down advice from the teachers and rational reflection on the personal learning process. On the one hand, lecturing may be an efficient way of teaching 200 students if talking in terms of 'how many students can we get through in three years'; but if taking a more intrinsic view of 'education in terms of changes in personal behaviour and attitudes, then one would say that that form of teaching is very inefficient indeed'. One participant made the following suggestion for achieving a balance between these two positions, even in mass lecturing:

One could start looking at the way in which we actually do impart information and ideas. Perhaps there is a lot more room for trying to construct lectures in a way in which you involve people in what you are trying to do. You scale down the amount of content that you give people and bring up the number of ideas and attitudes you want them to think about and work with... You initially take the lead and show them what you want them to do, but then it is up to them themselves to try to do it. If it is a question of getting them to think for themselves and to undertake activities which will change their attitudes and thinking about the world, then you don't need as much content. You need to think more about the process that is going on during the lecture hour.

However, the group saw the dilemma inherent in increasing student numbers and staff workload, and thus posing a temptation and danger of falling back on more conventional modes of teaching. Some academics had tried to challenge these constraints and to propose changes. 'But most people don't want change. How do you change that?'

## Change

My observation has been that real change in attitude and teaching behaviour is likely to occur not when imposed from outside, but when academics are actively involved in systematically reviewing their own practice. An institutional framework, such as a course approval system, may facilitate this review activity and process.

To be more specific, the action researchers in this study discussed two examples of the university course approval system as a mechanism to effect change and course improvement. Two of the participants conceded that they had initially resisted the 'high-handed verdict' and intimation that something needed to be changed in their courses. However, during and after the review in both cases, they changed their attitudes and teaching practice. They themselves (as action researchers) suggested and made substantial changes, so that the revised course outlines looked completely different from what they had been before. However, the changes were initiated, worked out and implemented by themselves. Both academics agreed, but pointed to the limitations of my theory as well.

## Limitations

One of the action researchers maintained that the above theory 'is only one way of looking at a very complex problem. You have asked people who are on your wavelength in terms of trying to improve the educational instruction of this university'.

Another academic who was unable to attend the meeting provided a similar comment in his letter:

> I suppose my first response is to wonder how much the high rating given to action research is a reflection of the predilections which led people into action research in the first place; your research may say more about a particular category of researchers than about action research as such.

With reference to Argyris and Schön (1974) we agreed that we are not living in a Model 2 world (characterised by openness, co-operation, advocacy with enquiry, evaluation with data, etc.). We do have to work with Model 1 people (characterised by unilateral decision-making, in control of tasks and others, advocacy without enquiry, withholding information, protecting self and others) who represent very strong forces in an institution.

I propose that it is possible to develop a Model 2 world; and that the people involved in it are saying that this is a desirable and effective way of working. For example, the participants in this study are Model 2 people who are open to innovation, change and continuous self-development. They rated action research highly, because it came closest to their personal theories of effective professional development.

However, the question was raised as to how other colleagues in the division who work within Model 1 would react to this repertory grid technique; how different their results would be; and whether and how it might be possible for them to change from a Model 1 to a Model 2 way of thinking. One possible avenue for effecting gradual change was seen in terms of working closely with individual colleagues or in small teams on a teaching or curriculum problem which directly concerns them, that is, which involves them actively in the solution of the problem, in revising and improving their practice systematically, and in writing up the conclusions of this action research. It was agreed that there was a need for further research and development in the area of change processes from Model 1 to Model 2 values and strategies.

The action researchers involved in these projects have influenced other colleagues through their activities in the realms of both administration and teaching. However, change has been slow and gradual; it has also been confronted by the resistance of those not sympathetic to the Model 2 approach. As one of the participants said: 'politics consumes a lot of our energy.' Yet, another commented: 'radicals and idealists have been too unpolitical in the past.' The development and eventual achievement of a Model 2 environment may thus require a far greater degree of political commitment and action on the part of the academics than has hitherto been the case. In this it can be seen that solutions to problems of staff development and student learning are not to be sought solely within the realm of higher education, whether in theory or practice, but within the domain of politics which impinges to such a significant degree on the realm of higher education.

## Conclusion

The purpose of this chapter was to present a case study of reflections on action research by the action researchers themselves. The study was based on a repertory grid and a group discussion of the grid results, as well as on general problems and the limitations of professional development.

On the whole, the action researchers' views of the nature of and criteria for effective professional development presented in this chapter coincide with my own theoretical framework (Zuber-Skerritt, 1992). Professional development is likely to be more effective if it involves a process of learning by experience, with active staff involvement in information-gathering and problem-solving; if it is personally and consciously initiated, thought out and implemented on the basis of their own needs, rather than controlled from outside.

This theory of professional development is difficult to operate in practice, because not all staff are self-motivated and interested in improving their teaching practice or, generally, in changing their attitudes and teaching behaviour. An institutional framework such as a university course approval system, coupled with an institutional environment in which good teaching is valued highly and supported by the power structure, were regarded as important influencing factors for all academics to develop the necessary intrinsic motivation and values for constantly improving their teaching practice. Moreover, a critical attitude and political action were considered necessary to counterbalance the forces within an institution guided by Model 1 values.

Whilst this chapter included the reflections of teaching academics on their action research, the following chapter will present my own reflections on action research from the perspective of an educational adviser, consultant or staff developer in higher education.

# Chapter 6

# Reflections on improving practice in higher education

### Introduction

The purpose of this chapter is to link the case studies in this book to the theoretical framework of the companion volume on *Professional Development in Higher Education* and to reflect upon the nature of action research in relation:

1. to student learning about their learning in an academic course or programme;
2. to staff learning about student learning; and
3. to my own learning about both of these areas.

To relate this chapter to the main arguments in the companion book, references to the theories and principles discussed in the book are provided as 'advance organisers' (in brief key terms and indicated in italics and brackets). Other references (e.g. to the case studies in this book) are also given (in brackets, but in normal type). This chapter reflects my action research on action research projects, using case study methodology. In other words, it is about action research on action research, or meta-action research.

The case is me, engaged in action research and reflecting on my practice as a staff development consultant working with faculty staff in the School of Modern Asian Studies (MAS) at Griffith University. I am not an objective, outside observer, but directly involved in the social world I am studying (*participant observation*). Therefore, my conclusions are necessarily my subjective interpretations of that particular social reality, although they may be tested by others in their particular educational context. I have a general set of principles guiding my practice and belonging to a theoretical framework developed in my companion book, but the research itself has been open and flexible. My interpretations have evolved through my views and perceptions of the staff and students in MAS. I have interpreted my specific experiences of my participation in and observation of action research projects in the social setting of MAS, while being part of it; and I had my interpretations confirmed by participants (*participant confirmation, triangulation*).

This chapter is structured along the lines of *The Action Research Planner* by Kemmis and McTaggart (1982), but it describes the action research spiral retrospectively. There are three major action steps in this case. The first step relates to action research into student learning in the MAS Foundation Programme and consists of a description of the first cycle. Although the teaching team went through several cycles after that (cf Chapter 2), the second step in my own research relates to action research with a different group of staff into postgraduate student learning in the MAS Master-by-Coursework Programme (cf Zuber-Skerritt and Rix, 1986). This second cycle was followed by another one pertaining to a different, but related problem in this programme. This cycle is not described in this chapter, but in Harris and Zuber-Skerritt (1986). The third action step in my research in this chapter also relates to action research into postgraduate student learning, but again with a different group of staff and students, namely in the MAS Honours Programme (cf Knight and Zuber-Skerritt, 1986; Zuber-Skerritt and Knight, 1985; 1986). Figure 7 is a diagrammatical representation of the three action steps.

After the description of this case of developing student learning skills at undergraduate and postgraduate levels, my reflections on the case follow in relation to the theories and models discussed in the companion book, especially to the CRASP model.

## The general idea

After several years of working as a senior consultant in the Centre for the Advancement of Learning and Teaching (CALT), I could see the advantages of the Griffith University course approval system to our work. It made it possible for the consultants in CALT to have a continuous impact on educational matters, the curriculum and on

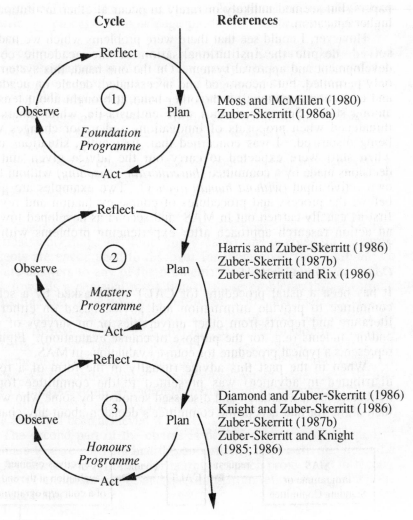

**Cycle**

**References**

Moss and McMillen (1980)
Zuber-Skerritt (1986a)

Harris and Zuber-Skerritt (1986)
Zuber-Skerritt (1987b)
Zuber-Skerritt and Rix (1986)

Diamond and Zuber-Skerritt (1986)
Knight and Zuber-Skerritt (1986)
Zuber-Skerritt (1987b)
Zuber-Skerritt and Knight
(1985;1986)

**Figure 7** *The spiral of action research into developing student learning skills*

academic staff. This became evident at national and international conferences, when staff developers from other units often seemed astonished at the progressiveness and innovative spirit of some MAS faculty staff and their concern for students' learning problems. This spirit and concern were implied in the reported work of the conference

83

papers, but seemed unlikely or rarely to occur at other institutions of higher education.

However, I could see that there were problems which we had not solved, despite the institutionalisation of the academic course development and approval system. On the one hand, this system not only permitted, but encouraged and necessitated, debate on academic and educational matters; on the other hand, it brought about tensions among staff. Some academics were enthusiastic, while others felt threatened when proposals of innovations and major changes were being discussed. I was concerned that, frequently, situations arose when staff were expected to carry out the advice given and the decisions made by a committee *(bureaucratic reasoning)* without their own active input *(without human agency)*. Two examples are given below: the process and procedures of course evaluation and review, first as usually carried out in MAS, and second as developed towards an action research approach after experiencing problems with the former procedures.

## Course evaluation in MAS

It has been a usual procedure for CALT to be asked by a school committee to provide information and advice based on either the literature and reports from other universities or on surveys of staff and/or students (e.g. for the purpose of course evaluation). Figure 8 represents a typical procedure for course evaluations in MAS.

When in the past this advice (usually in the form of a report distributed in advance) was presented to the committee for its deliberations, it was taken and discussed seriously by some who would then argue for and accept the committee's decision about any changes

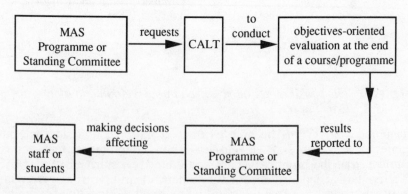

**Figure 8** *The traditional course evaluation/review in MAS*

to be made. There were others on the committee, however, who felt reluctant, threatened, defensive and hostile to the identified deficiencies of a course, to the proposed changes (which they would either ignore or pay mere lip service to) and to the CALT involvement in course development which they would regard as interfering with their teaching mode and routine *(Model 1 values)*. Quite understandably, members did not always fully comprehend the implications of the information, especially if it had been extracted in a brief form from several unit reports or from an extensive literature *(a problem of communication and language)*. Again, other members were sceptical or disturbed when research results challenged their own beliefs and practices *(a problem of paradigm)*. Some seemed bored and not interested at all in the case presented *(a problem of participation)*. It was often a matter of personal power and persuasion ability that led to a 'democratic' decision. If this tension existed among the committee members, it is not difficult to imagine (and to observe) how faculty staff felt, whose work was directly affected by these decisions Frustrated staff would complain that the whole debate and the committee work at Griffith University in general were a waste of time; such action was not sufficiently rewarded *(external values)* and it disadvantaged them in comparison with academics at other institutions of higher education who could do more research and 'get on with the job' rather than talking about it. Some even suggested the radical reduction of the committee structure to a minimum and the abolition of CALT. They argued that CALT faculty staff could be more useful, productive and 'cost-effective' to the institution *(bureaucratic rationality)* if they taught students in the schools. To sum up, on the one hand, many academics appreciated that the university's course approval system, with its built-in committee structure, did provide academic debate *(human agency in a critical community)* to ensure coherent degree programmes of high quality and responsible teaching; on the other hand, others were dissatisfied or objected to it.

Joint action research into curriculum development between MAS and CALT faculty staff seemed to be a possible solution to improve the situation, the practice of staff and their understanding of their practice. This became apparent in the following case study of a review of a new Main Study course.

*Course review as action research*

The review of this particular course — which cannot be named other than course X for reasons of confidentiality — must be seen against the background of the Griffith University course approval system. The first proposal (Submission I, explaining the rationale for mounting the course and its role, place and function within the school's overall programme) had been approved by all committees. The detailed proposal (Submission II, including the central question addressed, the aims, content, teaching methods, assessment rationale, items and weighting) was approved up to and including the school Standing Committee, but referred back to the school Standing Committee by the university's Education Committee with the following comments:

> the aims of the course... are couched in terms of what students will consider in the course, rather than what the objectives of the course are and how they will be achieved.

> the number of topics to be covered suggests that each topic can be given only limited attention. Furthermore it is difficult to see from the outline how the topics will be linked to present an integrated course on...X.

The school was requested to prepare a revised detailed outline in the light of these comments. A revised outline was submitted to the Chairman of the Education Committee who, in a subsequent memorandum, expressed his concern about the 'piecemeal' character of the proposed content, and the lack of integration, but 'approved the course subject to the condition that the school invited CALT to monitor the running of the course with a view to redesigning a more integrated course' for the subsequent year.

Although the convenor and teaching team disagreed 'profoundly' and objected to this 'high-handed verdict', the course convenor approached me as the representative of CALT. We both agreed that we would nevertheless proceed to conduct a review of this course — despite the unfortunate history of this ill-handled course approval — as we would have done anyway, without the Education Committee's attempted imposition, and as was the usual practice with newly run courses in MAS. We decided to invite the teaching team and a student representative to join in the review and to become full members of the review team. Thus the teaching/review team had to play the role of evaluators as well as critical self-evaluators conducting research into their own teaching *(the CRASP model)*. This course review as action research was different from previous practice when I (or another staff development colleague in CALT) conducted the evaluation/review, because it involved staff and student participation and decision-making.

The difference was that this review team decided that we would not only focus on finding out whether the stated objectives of the course had been achieved, but also allow for any additional aspects to emerge which might affect learning and teaching in this course and might even lead to a revision of the objectives *(a phenomenological and critical approach).* We would all observe the course *(participant observation),* decide on instant changes to be made during the operation of the course, ask students' and teaching staff's opinions of any positive and negative aspects of the course and of 'the learning milieu' and invite their suggestions for improvements *(illuminative evaluation).* Apart from this focus on the process of learning and teaching in this course seen from all of the participants' perspectives, we would analyse the assessment results at the end of the course with regard to students' knowledge and skills displayed *(outcomes)* and in comparison with other courses in the Main Study programme *(accountability).*

We used a variety of evaluation techniques: interviews (of individuals and groups); structured and unstructured discussions; a questionnaire with closed questions (based on the results of the structured group discussion) as well as open-ended questions (on the best and worst aspects of the course and whether it should be retained and why, or why not); document analysis; and assessment analysis. In the design of the review we made a conscious effort towards careful time management.

The time of teaching staff involvement was reduced as much as possible (i.e. to three review meetings, individual staff interviews of about 30 minutes each and filling in an open-ended questionnaire). We tried to avoid long student questionnaires which students would be reluctant to fill in, especially if they could not see instant improvements. Instead we obtained useful feedback from students by conducting structured group discussions of one hour each: the Nominal Group Technique and a Questionnaire Based Discussion. We delegated all time-consuming tasks (e.g. writing summaries of interviews and of evaluative discussions, minutes of review meetings, memoranda, interim reports, etc.) to (three different) staff members (and a visitor) in CALT. The summaries of the staff interviews were distributed to and confirmed by each teaching academic concerned before they were presented to the second review meeting *(respondent confirmation).* At this meeting the results of the evaluative discussions with students were also discussed, some of which led to instant improvements; others required long-term changes. The results of staff's and students' opinions of the whole course were discussed in the final review meeting. By the end of this meeting the team had resolved to make substantial changes to the course.

The changes made had already been requested by the Education Committee; however, the review team did not arrive at its decisions by following or even keeping in mind the committee's concerns, but through its own research into staff and students' opinions of the course. It was also resolved to communicate these decisions in form of a revised 'Detailed Course Outline' and a report from the course convenor to the Academic Committee via the school Standing Committee. As a result, both the school's and the university's approval committees accepted the revisions; but in addition, both the teaching team and the students in this course were satisfied. Although students had indicated midway through the course in their surveys and discussions that by comparison to other courses this was a particularly difficult and demanding course because of its highly theoretical content, the assessment analysis showed that students' average results in this course were higher than in other Main Study courses and higher than the same students' results in other courses. It is worth mentioning that all assessment items in this course were double-marked.

## *Reflections*

In the university's course approval system, an explanation is required of the aims of a course and how the teaching team intends to achieve those aims. A course review is, therefore, assumed to be aims-and-objectives-oriented and may be conducted by an outside researcher. The experience of action research in this course review, as described in the above case study, showed that this kind of review activity by the academics themselves not only confirmed that the intended aims had been achieved, but that in the process other problems which would otherwise not have been discovered until well after the end of the review were eliminated. It could also be observed that the teaching staff, throughout the review and in the review meetings, felt directly involved and responsible for improving the course to the students' satisfaction as well as their own. The student representative on the review team constantly reminded us of students' difficulties and needs and interpreted their comments.

Experiences such as this gave me the idea that being in the action field of a course review provides teaching staff with a deeper understanding of the whole situation — with a greater awareness of how student problems can arise and be solved; with the realisation of the need for continuous evaluation, self-evaluation, self-reflection and change; and, as a result, with professional development *(the CRASP model)*. Within the course approval system, teaching staff are more likely to display a professional attitude if they are personally involved in designing and reviewing the courses they have to teach and they are more able to criticise and change the context in which they work, if necessary *(emancipatory action research)*. Specifically, they are more capable to change and adjust their practice if they are actively involved in identifying, analysing and solving the problems hidden in their practice *(experiential learning)*, rather than having this research done for them. So my strategic action was to try to encourage MAS faculty staff to engage in educational action research into those problems of learning and teaching which were foremost in their minds.

## Field of action in the substantive context

The field of action I have chosen for my case study of action research in higher education in this chapter is the development of student learning skills at both undergraduate and postgraduate levels in the substantive context of the School of MAS (cf Chapters 2 and 3).

One of the major problems facing teachers in higher education in the last two or three decades has been an increasingly heterogeneous student population with varying degrees of knowledge and basic skills. The question of how to help students develop their learning skills has been a pressing one since the late 70s in MAS, especially because of a shortage of enrolments and a need to prevent high drop-out rates. Although many staff members could see the necessity of becoming more student-oriented in their approach, they did not see themselves qualified or having the time to teach study skills such as essay writing, reading, presenting a paper, etc. in a systematic way. They assumed that this would be the task of 'experts' outside MAS (e.g. CALT staff, the Student Counsellor or specially hired tutors). All of these possibilities were explored. Faculty staff in both MAS and CALT perceived the issue of developing student learning and research skills as of foremost importance, because many other issues and problems, such as high failure and drop-out rates, seemed to be related to this issue; but the staff of neither felt directly responsible for teaching these skills. CALT's terms of reference do not include teaching undergraduate students, but only improving student learning through curriculum development and working with faculty staff. Faculty staff in MAS saw their role in teaching subject matter, not remedial teaching of basic skills (i.e. undergraduate study skills which should have been acquired at high school and postgraduate research skills which should have been developed at undergraduate level). Another major constraint was that the school's budget did not allow for enough resources to mount a proper programme. Thus, on the one hand, there was a clearly identified need to teach study and research skills, on the other, there were the constraints of having to operate under normal conditions without extra resources and staff.

Initial attempts to offer lectures on essay writing, oral communication, the use of the library, speed reading sessions, etc. by outside 'experts' in student learning seemed unsatisfactory, because those students who were in most need would not attend, and many of those who did were bored and could not always see the direct relevance of the lectures or other sessions to their own coursework. It became obvious from staff and students' responses that the ideal solution would be a systematic course on study or research skills which would be fully integrated into the content and timetable of the particular degree programme and designed not as a remedial course, but as a series of workshops in which students could find out how they themselves learn, how others learn and discuss desirable changes to be made in their learning as individuals and as a group (e.g. in tutorials).

I intended to try out three main strategies of action. First, I would join the teaching team in designing, conducting and reviewing a workshop component integrated into the particular programme. This would give me an opportunity to study and understand the issue better in its substantive social and political context, and I could assist teaching staff directly in their practice. Second, I would suggest to the convenors of the particular programmes that they do action research into this issue by 'planning, acting, observing and reflecting' on each workshop. Third, I would suggest to them to write:

1. a report to the Undergraduate Programme Committee or Postgraduate Board summarising the whole experience and making recommendations for the future; and
2. a journal article, because of the paucity of research in this area of higher education at the time.

The first step in the spiral of my action research is the development of a workshop component in the MAS Foundation Course (cf Figure 9).

## The first action step: developing learning skills in the MAS Foundation Course

The rationale, aims, content, methods and review of the workshop component on student learning skills as an integrated part of the first year programme in MAS are described in detail in Chapter 2. Therefore they are not included in this section.

*Plan*

My own action plan can be followed in the diagram in Figure 9. The opportunities to implement my action plan were very favourable because all four groups of people concerned about the issue were interested in finding a solution. First, in CALT I received research assistance with a survey of all higher education institutions in Australia and New Zealand as to their practices of developing student learning skills; with collating the selected materials from other institutions for MAS students as *Guidelines on Student Learning Skills* (Zuber-Skerritt

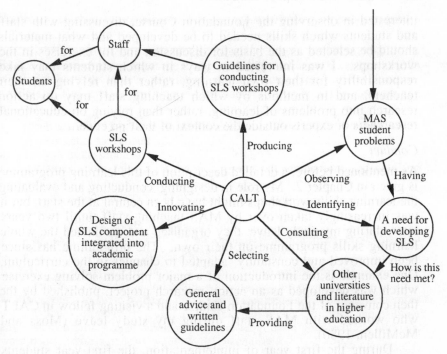

**Figure 9** *An action plan for developing student learning skills (SLS) in a first-year programme*

and Cunningham, 1986); with surveys of staff and student opinions; and with report writing. Second, MAS students were keen to develop their skills. According to their survey responses, their attendance of workshops was between 80 and 100 per cent. There were also enough student volunteers to participate in feedback sessions, such as Nominal Group and Questionnaire-Based Discussions, and filling in questionnaires. Third, the convenor and teaching team of the MAS Foundation Course welcomed and appreciated CALT's assistance in a new and fuzzy area of their teaching responsibilities. All of them participated in a staff workshop on developing student discussion skills (Zuber-Skerritt, 1986b) at the beginning of the academic year. This topic was chosen because it is most important for leaders of workshops and tutorials to realise what the supportive and the destructive elements in a discussion group are; and because it is most difficult for academics to learn to be facilitators of student discussion and learning, rather than lecturers *(a shift from Model 1 to Model 2)*. Finally, I was personally interested in observing the Foundation Course, discussing with staff and students which skills needed to be developed and what materials should be selected as the basis for discussion and for exercises in the workshops. I was interested in ways in which students may take responsibility for their own learning, rather than relying on their teachers, and in methods by which teaching staff may do action research into problems of learning, rather than relying on educational researchers or experts outside the context of their practice.

## Conduct

As mentioned before, a detailed description of this learning programme is given in Chapter 2. My role in designing, conducting and evaluating the learning skills workshops might have been central at the start, but it was increasingly taken over by MAS teaching staff, until two years later, during my study leave, they organised and conducted the whole learning skills programme on their own. The programme has since been improved and constantly adapted to changes in the curriculum. One example is the introduction of a major problem-solving exercise which was developed as an action research project, published by the then convenor of the Foundation Course and a visiting fellow in CALT who worked with MAS staff during my study leave (Moss and McMillen, 1980).

During the first year of implementation, the first-year students were divided into four workshop groups. I conducted each workshop in the series with one group of students, while the other three groups were taken by three different academics in MAS who would first observe my session before conducting their own in order to get a feeling for the situation and to anticipate students' reactions to the planned questions and tasks. The whole learning skills programme was mainly monitored by CALT staff. The summaries of feedback sessions and questionnaires provided the teaching team with information and impressions necessary for reflection and revision. This knowledge of what happened provided the basis for the improvement of the strategic plan and action in subsequent cycles.

## Reflections

My own reflections on this action research spiral led me to conclude that all people involved in this project of developing student learning skills in the Foundation Course (i.e. students, teaching staff and myself) learnt from this experience. The students became aware of their own and others' strategies and processes of learning and what and how to change from then on. They realised that they had the ability and responsibility to constantly develop and revise their learning skills.

The university teachers who conducted, observed and listened to the discussions experienced a heightened understanding of their students' problems of learning the subject matter. For example, students would mention constraints of the course which impeded meaningful learning (e.g. the workload was too high; students did not have enough time to read for tutorials; the tutorial papers were too long and boring, so students stopped attending, because there was not sufficient opportunity to participate actively in fruitful discussion). In this way, staff became more aware of students' difficulties, needs and learning styles, and many of them, consciously or unconsciously, changed from a lecturer-centred to a more student-oriented approach to teaching which could be observed in subsequent sessions. I (as a staff development adviser) realised that the teachers — like students — learnt best 'by doing', through personal experience, problem-solving or discussion in a non-threatening environment, rather than by being told what to do and how to do it to achieve given aims *(personal scientists, problem solvers and agents, rather than respondents)*. They were not hostile to this new development and the changes in the curriculum because they were actively engaged in, and felt responsible for, the design and development of the innovation. This insight has had implications for my role and work as a consultant in higher education: since then I have tried to design situations and use strategies which facilitate the teachers' own active enquiry into their practice, and I have tried to pose questions to them as a critical friend, rather than providing the answers and suggesting solutions to the problems arising in their practice.

However, there were some difficulties with this case study which should be avoided in the next action research cycle. First, students' feedback suggested that they were not clear about the aims of the workshops and how these related to their coursework; an introductory lecture and a written outline of the whole series could alleviate this problem. Students could also then have the opportunity to respond to the planned programme and suggest changes, if necessary. Second, teaching staff were not sufficiently involved in the research, monitoring and report writing of this new development; they only discussed the results presented by CALT. Writing a final report to the relevant committee or board responsible for course reviews might crystallise their own views and formulate them for other practitioners or review teams in the future. Third, there were too many workshops in this series, often following one another too closely, so that I had time to make only cursory notes which I sometimes supplemented later with fuller accounts. Ideally, one should have completed the notes from the previous workshop and discussed them with the teaching team before teaching and observing the next. Although the teaching team has since gone through several cycles of replanning, acting, observing and reflecting, with and without my participation, a more stringent record system could be kept of all meetings, evaluative discussions by students and staff and of their own reflections in a diary. However, it would be unrealistic to expect this of teaching staff who are involved in several courses and in reviews of those courses. That is why assistance from a unit like CALT can be useful, if it is facilitative but not dominating. I kept these points in mind in the second step of my action research on action research (cf Figure 7).

## The second action step: developing dissertation research and writing skills in the MAS Master-by-Coursework programme

As in the previous case study, the aims, content, methods and review of this learning programme for postgraduate students are not described in detail in this section, because they are included in Chapter 3 and in Zuber-Skerritt and Rix (1986) and Harris and Zuber-Skerritt(1986). The idea of conducting this study emerged from the MAS Postgraduate Coursework Board that discussed student problems of dissertation research and writing (in the part-time Master-by-Coursework Programme) on the basis of examiners' reports, the university's dissatisfaction with late submissions of dissertations and students' apparent lack of skills in research, especially in methodology and dissertation writing. My question to the board as to how students were helped to develop those required skills in the programme received diverse reactions. On the one side, members admitted that little was done and that they thought something should be done; on the other side, one member believed that students who could not cope with the requirements of the dissertation should not be in this programme, even if it meant that the whole programme had to be abolished, for it was the responsibility of university academics to teach postgraduate students the subject matter, not how to go about writing a thesis. However, the convenor of this programme had heard of the learning skills component in the Foundation Course and was keen to mount a similar component at the postgraduate level for his students with the assistance of CALT.

### Plan

In order to avoid conflict over this issue, it was important to have a contract with the board which allowed us to not only design and conduct a workshop component on dissertation research and writing as a trial, but subsequently to integrate the component into the structure and content of the whole programme if and on the condition that the trial was monitored and proved to be successful. My action plan is summarised in Figure 10.

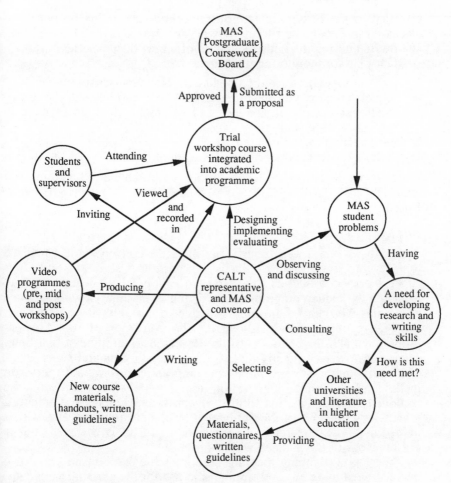

**Figure 10** *An action plan for developing student dissertation research and writing skills in a Master-by-Coursework programme*

A first step was to consult the sparse literature in this field which showed that our students' problems were not unique, but experienced by students elsewhere, even by full-time PhD students. The reported problems and reasons for students' discontinuation or late submission of their theses provided a good argument for accepting the problems in MAS as more or less 'normal' and for trying to alleviate them by a proposal to the Postgraduate Coursework Board. This proposal, as discussed in Zuber-Skerritt and Rix (1986), was accepted by the board and revised during the implementation of the workshop series.

Our plan for monitoring the course was:

1. to obtain feedback from both students and supervisors by means of a questionnaire with open-ended questions and through the use of video recordings of at least one session and of an evaluative discussion at the end;
2. participant observation; and
3. an analysis of the dissertation assessment.

We also planned to write a full report (with appended handouts and materials used in the workshops) to the Postgraduate Coursework Board.

## *Conduct*

Although we had a well thought-out plan, the convenor and I realised that it was important to discuss it with the students and their supervisors, who attended the first workshop. This discussion was triggered by a video programme consisting of my interviews with three academics who played an important role in postgraduate supervision: the Dean of the School of MAS, the convenor of this Masters programme and the chairman of the Research Committee at that time. Their views were critically discussed by the students and supervisors, especially their views on the role and functions of a supervisor, methods of developing dissertation research and writing skills and the responsibility for the final draft. Everyone developed a standpoint, which we collected in the form of a brief questionnaire and which helped us in our research and understanding of the issues as well as in our revisions of the planned workshops.

We had a planning meeting before each workshop, in which we decided what materials and strategies to use for the particular topic and skill to be developed and who would play which role. Since there was only one group of students (in contrast to the Foundation Course), we conducted each workshop jointly; and since we were both actively involved in either teaching or observing, we subsequently compared our observation notes taken during and after the session and discussed the implications for a revision of our plan of the next workshop.

## *Reflections*

Although the evaluation results of this workshop component were very positive from both the students' and supervisors' points of view, and although the component was approved by the board and established as an integral part of the degree programme, there were negative as well as positive effects. To start with, the positive effects refer to the participants' learning experiences. Among other comments, students stated that they learnt to organise their work better and that they discovered with fellow students and staff some of their problems. They appreciated the support from and interaction with staff and students. Supervisors commented that they appreciated the workshops as thought-provoking, systematic, non-threatening, and as a framework for themselves and students to work from. The convenor and I learnt from this whole experience and from writing the report to the board, as well as presenting a revised version of it to an international conference and then to an international journal of higher education. I concluded that it was worthwhile making the extra effort of rewriting an internal report for presentation to an external audience, not only for my own satisfaction *(and accountability)*, but also for that of academics and their confidence as action researchers in higher education.

However, there were also three main negative aspects which concerned me. First, two out of ten academics who participated in at least some of the workshops commented that the sessions were too time consuming and that some of the discussions could have been shortened by distributing written guidelines *(bureaucratic rationality)*. The students and staff who participated in the final video-recorded evaluative discussion and who had attended all workshops disagreed with this view and stated that the sessions not only helped students develop the intended skills, but also contributed to their increased motivation, self-confidence and understanding of other people's views and difficulties, and that these unintended aims had been very valuable and could not have been achieved by individual supervision and written advice alone *(but by human agency)*. If we had not heard these comments and if we had not monitored this workshop course carefully, we might have been discouraged by the earlier staff comments on the costs of time. It is difficult enough to argue, as it is, that values gained by the process of critical and self-reflective discussion and debate *(internal goods)* should outweigh considerations of effectiveness of time and resources *(external goods)*. As one of the supervisors argued, if staff had not attended these sessions which were scheduled from 5.30–8.30 pm, it would not have cost the university any more or less. It is part of academic freedom and responsibility to engage in long and developmental discussions.

My second concern was that some supervisors fell into the old habit of lecturing and dominating the discussion instead of probing students' thoughts. On the one hand, students commented that they appreciated the opportunity of listening to other supervisors' views; on

97

the other hand, our aim was to provide them with the chance to reflect upon, formulate and develop their own views through active discussion. It is one of the most difficult tasks to make academic staff understand this aim and to act accordingly.

Third, the emphasis in this workshop course was on the 'nuts and bolts' of social science research and on the process and main problems of dissertation writing, rather than on the students' underlying assumptions which determined their methods. It would have been too ambitious in such a vocation-oriented coursework programme (60 per cent courses, 40 per cent dissertation) to do otherwise, especially since the focus of the programme was not on the philosophy of social science, but on the practical politics and economics of 'Australian–Asian Relations'. However, a postgraduate research-oriented programme should allocate a full-semester (or full-year) course on the problems as well as the methods of research, as discussed in the next action step.

## The third action step: developing research skills in the MAS Honours programme

This action step consisted of four loops. The first loop was a revision of an existing MAS Honours course entitled 'Problems and Methods in Research'. This revision was requested by the Honours Board on the basis of staff tensions and some students' complaints about the ideological bias of the course, but it was conducted by CALT in close collaboration with the convenor and the teaching team, because by that time I had learnt that real changes would be implemented only if they were the result of the practitioners' own action research, rather than the conclusion of an outside investigation. It should be noted that this course had been introduced in 1980 and was also taught in 1981 before it was revised and taught by a different team under a different convenorship in 1982. The review in the first loop of this action research spiral occurred at the end of 1983 and was reported to and considered by the Honours Board at the beginning of the academic year in 1984, when the second loop started.

The second loop was a revision of this revised course, but initiated by the course convenor, who was interested in observing the effects of the new course with all its changes on the students' work and on the staff–student interactions. As a result of this action research cycle which included innovations similar to those in the previous action step, we went through two further loops. However, the emphasis was on the reflection phase, based on the observation of action in the first two loops.

*Plan*

The action plan for these four loops can be summarised in diagrammatical form as shown in Figures 11.1 and 11.2 .

The first review imposed by the Honours Board was politically difficult and could have been disastrous if it had been conducted in an authoritarian 'expert' manner (Figure 8) and if the teaching team had resisted an open enquiry into the course and subsequent foisted changes. Fortunately, it was in the nature of this course that all three members of the teaching team were in favour of constant, open, critical enquiry into any social practice, because they were teaching students the ideas of non-positivist, critical theory in the social sciences as part of the course *(Paradigm 2)*. On the contrary, their self-reflection and enthusiasm for critical debate about their practice grew from loop to loop.

*Conduct*

The survey in the first loop (cf Figure 11.1 (a)) was conducted by a postal, open-ended questionnaire inviting all MAS Honours students (1980–1983) to assist the MAS Honours Board in identifying problem areas and making changes for improvement. The questionnaire was structured around the following headings:

1. What did you like best about this course?
2. What did you like least about this course?
3. What suggestions for improvement would you make?

The responses of students enrolled in 1980–81 were separated from those enrolled in 1982–83 because the course had changed substantially, e.g. from a positivist to a non-positivist approach. Most of the changes recommended by the former group of students had already been made since 1982; others which had not been incorporated yet were reiterated by the students enrolled in 1982–83. On the whole, students' opinions of the course were much more positive than one would have expected from the rumours and the students' petitions in 1983. All students (except one) made positive comments and constructive suggestions for improvement. Some considered the course to be essential for Honours students; others thought it was too late, but would have liked more exposure to research methods in their undergraduate courses to better prepare them for this Honours course. I discussed these criticisms and suggestions for improvement with the convenor and the teaching team before writing my report and presentingmy recommendations to the Honours Board. These jointly agreed-upon recommendations related to:

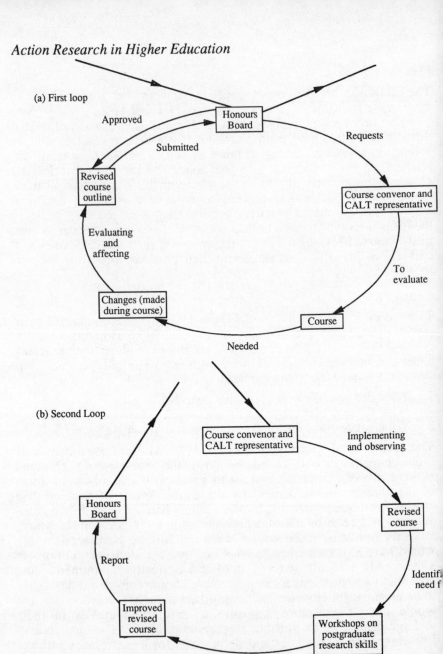

**Figure 11.1**   *An action plan for reviewing a course on 'Problems and Methods in Research' (Part 1)*

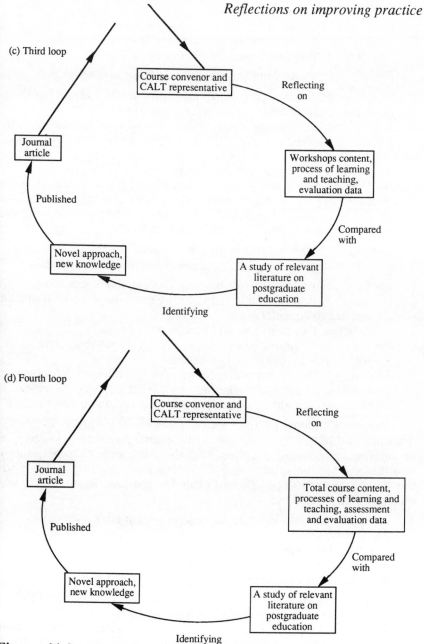

**Figure 11.2** *An action plan for reviewing a course on 'Problems and Methods in Research' (Part 2)*

1. immediate improvements by the teaching team in 1984; and
2. long-term considerations by the School of MAS.

   For example, immediate improvements recommended were:

1. reducing the number of lectures on Althusser and replacing them by in-depth discussion of other alternative approaches;
2. making the terminology easier for students to understand (e.g. by providing handouts — definitions of terms, examples of concepts, etc.);
3. offering a workshop on thesis writing;
4. considering individual students' thesis topics and trying to show relationships and linkages between lectures and text readings on the one side, and the practical theses on the other, thus making the lectures more relevant to the individual projects.

Long-term considerations by the School of MAS (after the intended review in 1984, and in the light of its results) included:

1. teaching team to consider changes to content and assessment;
2. Honours Board, Main Study Sub-Committee and Standing Committee to consider:
   (a) whether this course should be compulsory; and
   (b) whether it should be offered to third year students instead of, or as well as, to Honours students.
3. The above three committees and the Foundation Programme Committee to consider whether, and what aspects of, research methodology should be integrated into undergraduate courses.

The second loop of this action research (cf Figure 11.1 (b)) occurred in 1984, when I observed all lectures, reading sessions (i.e. discussion of provided excerpts of documents and other materials), tutorials and seminars, and when I conducted a workshop jointly with the course convenor on 'Dissertation Design and Rationale'. We monitored the course by:

1. evaluative discussions with the teaching team after each class;
2. my observation notes;
3. informal discussions with students;
4. video-recording of the workshop; and
5. an open-ended questionnaire at the end of the course.

As in the first loop, I wrote a final report to the Honours Board after discussing and revising the first draft with the convenor.

The third loop (cf Figure 11.2 (c)) was based on the action observed in two workshops, the one on problem definition ('Dissertation Design and Rationale' introduced in the second loop) and the other workshop on 'Thesis Writing' which we introduced in the course in 1985. We obtained feedback on this second workshop by audio-recording of students' comments and of an interview with one member of the teaching team who had attended the session. An in-depth reflection on the content, the processes of learning and teaching and on the evaluation data of both workshops in comparison with findings in the existing literature on postgraduate education led us to the conclusion that our experiences and personal theories might be of interest to other teachers in higher education and to staff developers engaged in postgraduate education. Therefore, we published two papers, one short and one full-length article (Zuber-Skerritt and Knight, 1985; 1986).

The fourth loop (cf Figure 11.2 (d)) was again an in-depth reflection, this time on the total course content, the processes of learning and teaching, the assessment and the evaluation data collected and recorded in the previous three loops. When comparing our experiences and insights gained in this action research on developing research skills in honours students against the findings in the literature on postgraduate education, we identified some aspects of our approach which seemed novel and of interest to other teachers and staff developers in higher education. Therefore we presented a paper to the HERDSA Conference (Higher Education Research and Development Society of Australasia) in 1985 which was published in its proceedings and, in a revised form, in its journal in 1986.

## Reflections

I consider this last step of my whole action research project as the most successful. It may be called 'emancipatory' action research in Carr and Kemmis' (1986) terms, because it fulfils the three requirements of action research in that the action in the course reviews was 'strategic' (i.e. deliberate and controlled by the action researchers) rather than technical or habitual; the action researchers proceeded through a spiral of planning, acting, observing and reflecting; and they participated and collaborated in all phases of the research activity.

Another criterion for success may be that the results have been accepted as valid educational research and published by internationally renowned journals of higher education. In particular, the paper on 'Problem Definition and Thesis Writing' (Zuber-Skerritt and Knight, 1986), has aroused interest and enquiries from all over the world (especially from Third World countries) with requests for other papers, reports and video programmes.

103

## Limitations of the case

Action research is time consuming. We had to operate under normal conditions (i.e. without additional resources and staff). Teaching staff were intrinsically motivated to spend extra time on researching and improving their practice. The Griffith University course approval system may facilitate an enquiry, but it does not guarantee that the enquiry will transform practice and the practitioners' understanding of the practice, especially if the enquiry is being conducted by CALT staff alone. This book has argued that educational practice is more likely to be improved if the conditions, theories and principles for improvement have been discovered by the teachers who have to put them into practice. The time spent on solving problems in the curriculum and in the practice of learning and teaching should be considered as part of the normal duties of a teacher in higher education, but often it is not. Emancipatory action research requires even more time, for it not only improves practice but, as Car and Kemmis (1986, 169) put it:

> Action research helps practitioners to theorise their practice, to revise their theories self-critically in the light of practice, and to transform their practice into praxis (informed, committed action).

Theorising and the group process of deliberation take time, yet they are the very essence of the academics' activities, not only in their disciplinary research, but also in their teaching. The difficulty is to convince academics of this ideal. The bureaucratic argument of time and cost efficiency is hard to beat. For example, it could be argued that it would have been much faster if the teaching team of course X in the case study described above in this chapter had followed the Education Committee's advice to streamline the course and make it into a more integrated, coherent whole, instead of conducting a time-consuming review with practically the same results. However, it would be dangerous if academics adopted a merely technical role and carried out institutional advice, instead of critically testing whether the assumptions behind that advice and the advice itself are appropriate to the particular case. The teaching team of course X arrived at their own conclusions through experience, critical reflection and self-reflection. They made the problem of integration as well as the solution to the problem their own. Ever since, they have continued the debate on the content of this highly controversial, ideological course; they have sought students' opinions, and made changes, especially since there have been staff changes.

Writing a report or paper at the end of an action research project also takes time, although it has the advantage that ideas are crystallised and that records are kept of the professional achievements of the practitioners involved. It is only after teaching academics have experienced action research themselves that they can judge whether the advantages outweigh the disadvantages, as discussed in the previous chapter.

Another limitation of this case might be that only the course convenors participated in the writing of the reports/papers. Other members of the teaching teams contributed with their observations, evaluative comments and suggestions for improvement, but they were not actively involved in writing, an activity which is most developmental. Methods of involving the whole team in the writing process would be a challenge for further development and research.

Finally, this case has its limitations when it comes to validity. Critics of participant observation and of illuminative evaluation may decry this case study of action research in higher education as subjective, biased, impressionistic and lacking precision and quantifiable measures, all of which are negative characteristics in experimental research *(in the normative, positivist paradigm 1)*. However, these positivist criteria are inappropriate in judging this work. I did not set out to be objective, unbiased and to use quantifiable measures in order to control variables and predict precise, behavioural practice elsewhere. I am not claiming the universal truth of my deductions from this case. I have been concerned with explaining and interpreting human action as behaviour-with-meaning and as the source of personal and social knowledge building *(in the interpretive, non-positivist paradigm 2)*. Theory has emerged from particular situations; it has been 'grounded' in the data generated by action researchers and has therefore made sense to those to whom it applies. Although I have checked and negotiated my interpretations with the participants in this case study in critical discussions and mutual 'learning conversations', the validity of these interpretations only applies to this case. It is up to other action researchers to show whether these grounded theories are valid in their own educational contexts.

## Reflections on the case

The aim of this section is to reflect on the implications of this case study (on developing student learning and research skills) for the praxis of higher education. The praxis described in this part is *not* the result of a conscious application of existing theories, but it has been developed independently. At the most I have been influenced by my tacit knowledge of certain theories, but I have read most of them after the development of this case in practice and I then recognised their relevance to this kind of action research. In the companion book I show the connections between certain theories and practices by reconstructing those ideas and models which are coherent with the action research described in this book. For example, I reflect on this case of action research into student learning and research skills with respect to:

1. Kelly's personal construct theory;
2. Leontiev's action theory;
3. critical education science; and
4. the CRASP model.

## Conclusion

In this chapter I have tried to show the relationship of the case studies in this book to the theories in the companion book by means of a case study of my own action research into my practice as a senior consultant in higher education. In presenting my action research, I followed the normal cycles: plan–conduct (i.e. act and observe)–reflect.

The general idea of encouraging academics to do action research into their own teaching practice arose from my concerns in my own practice and from deficiencies in the system of course evaluations which I was requested to conduct on behalf of the School of MAS. I concluded from my observation of course evaluations and reviews that teaching staff are more likely to make substantive changes to their practice if they are actively involved in identifying, analysing and solving the problems in the curriculum and in student learning (cf the case of course X), rather than having this research done for them (cf Figure 8).

The field of action chosen was the development of student learning skills at both undergraduate and postgraduate levels, because this seemed to be an important, controversial and new issue not only in the School of MAS, but also in other institutions in Australia, Britain and elsewhere.

The spiral of my action research consisted of three major steps or cycles, each in turn consisting of several cycles or loops again. In these three steps the development of student learning, of staff learning and of my own learning became apparent. Each step referred to action research projects (described in Chapters 2 and 3) in the MAS Foundation Course, the Master-by-Coursework programme and the Honours programme (cf the overview in Figure 7).

My reflections on this case lead me to the conclusion that my role as an educational adviser in higher education is not so much to provide information, advice and the results of evaluation and research to teaching staff who would then apply this knowledge to their practice, but to help them to create this knowledge themselves through experience, self-reflection and critical debate with others. Similarly, the role of teaching staff is not so much to provide students with the answers of their research in a particular field, but with questions which give them the opportunity to discover the answers themselves through problem-solving and discussion with their fellow students and staff.

However, I have also indicated the limitations of this case. The main problem is to make staff realise that their arguments about time constraints and about a lack of institutional rewards *(external values)* for educational action research activities are bureaucratic and self-defeating. Unless academics control their own practice as true professionals, displaying a critical, enquiring attitude, researching and justifying the academic value of their practice through continuing self-evaluation and professional development *(the CRASP model)*, their own existence and that of their institution will be jeopardised through outside control.

# Conclusions

This book has presented several examples of action research in higher education which demonstrate that the practice of learning, teaching and educational development can be improved by collaborative enquiry of academics and their staff development colleagues into problems of student learning or curriculum development in higher education.

This enquiry can be described as emancipated action research if it meets the following requirements: it proceeds through the spiral of action research cycles each consisting of planning, acting, observing and reflecting; and it involves participation, collaboration and group decision in all phases of the research activity. According to the CRASP model (cf Table 3), action research is:

*Critical* (and self-critical) *collaborative* enquiry by
*Reflective* teachers in higher education being
*Accountable* and making the results of their enquiry public,
*Self-evaluating* their practice and engaged in
*Participatory* problem-solving and continuing professional development.

The examples of developments in student learning skills at both the undergraduate and postgraduate levels addressed an important, controversial and new issue not only for Griffith University, but also for other institutions of higher education in Australia, Britain and other countries.

The public concern for effectiveness and efficiency in higher education in recent years (including student retention and completion rates) and increasing government pressures for accountability have caused a great deal of anxiety and a crisis in higher education. Action research offers a positive, constructive solution to these problems in that it provides a framework and methodology for self- and peer-appraisal, evaluation, improvement and development in a supportive and formative environment on a voluntary basis. The participants themselves can then decide to publish the results and submit them for consideration (e.g. by committees responsible for decisions on probation, promotion, tenure, etc.).

The advantages of emancipatory action research in higher education, if carried out properly, are:

- the improvement of learning and teaching practice;
- the participants' enhanced understanding of their practice;
- critical analysis and change of conditions impeding desirable improvements and further development;
- professional development of teachers in higher education;
- the advancement of knowledge and grounded theory;
- accountability to the institution and to the community at large;
- rewards for evidence of quality teaching and research publications;
- greater job satisfaction.

My reflections on action research in this volume lead me to three major conclusions.

1. Teaching staff are more likely to make substantive changes to their practice if they are actively involved in identifying, analysing and solving the problems in the curriculum and in student learning, rather than having this research done for them.
2. The role of academic development staff is not so much to provide information, advice and the results of evaluation and research to faculty staff who would then apply this knowledge to their practice, but to assist them in creating this knowledge themselves through experience, self-reflection and critical debate with others.
3. Similarly, the role of teaching staff in higher education is not so much to provide students with the answers of research in a particular field, but with questions giving them the opportunity to discover the answers themselves through problem-solving and discussion with their fellow students and staff.

However, there are also limitations to the use of action learning and action research in higher education. There are situations in which collaborative enquiry is inappropriate, because it would be too time-consuming compared with other methods leading to the same results; for example, if the answers to a problem are already known and are either right or wrong; if knowledge is programmable (e.g. computer packages) or if it can be obtained faster by other means. Thus action research is not the panacea for all problems, but it is appropriate in an uncertain environment for solving problems in complex situations in which the answers are not simple or known to be right or wrong.

Other limitations might be perceived by teaching staff who argue that collaborative enquiry into learning and teaching problems is disadvantageous because of time constraints and a lack of institutional rewards for educational action research activities. However, this argument is bureaucratic and self-defeating. Unless teachers in higher education control their own practice as true professionals displaying a critical, enquiring attitude, researching and justifying the academic value of their practice through continuing self-evaluation and professional development (i.e. the CRASP model), their own existence and that of their institution are jeopardised through outside control.

For this reason, there is a need and scope for further research and continuing development in the area of improving practice in higher education. I hope that this volume will stimulate many academics and staff developers to follow a similar path to that shown in the examples of action research detailed in this volume and those in my previous book, *Action Research for Change and Development* (1991).

A theoretical framework is presented in the companion book, entitled *Professional Development in Higher Education — A Theoretical Framework for Action Research* (1992).

# References

Adie, H., Fairbrother, F. and Zuber-Skerritt, O. (1986) Excellence in university teaching — a new staff development programme, *Proceedings of the Twelfth International Conference on Improving University Teaching*, Heidelberg, 603-19.

Argyris, C. (1980) *Inner Contradictions of Rigorous Research*, Academic Press, London.

Argyris, C. and Schön, D. (1974) *Theory in Practice: Increasing Professional Effectiveness*, Jossey-Bass, San Francisco.

Ballard, B. and Clanchy, J. (1984) *Study Abroad — A Manual for Asian Students*, Longman, London.

Barrett, E. and Magin, D. (1983) *Postgraduate Degrees: How Long Do They Really Take?* Occasional Publication 23, TERC, University of New South Wales, Sydney.

Beard, R. and Hartley, J. (1984) *Teaching and Learning in Higher Education* (Fourth Edition), Harper and Row, London.

Bligh, D.A. (1972) *What's the Use of Lectures?* Penguin, Harmondsworth.

Bloom, B.S. (1956) *Taxonomy of Educational Objectives. Handbook 1: Cognitive Domain*, McKay, New York.

Bridgestock, M. and Backhouse, D. (1982) Improving attendance and participation by science students in Science, Technology and Society tutorials: a psychologically based approach, *Studies in Higher Education* 7 (2), 153-58.

Bruner, J.S. (1975) Beyond the information given, in N. Entwistle and D. Hounsell (eds) *How Students Learn*, University of Lancaster, Lancaster, 105-16.

Carr, W. and Kemmis, S. (1986) *Becoming Critical: Education, Knowledge and Action Research*, Falmer Press, Basingstoke, Hants.

Connell, R.W. (1985) How to supervise a PhD, *Vestes* 28 (2), 38-41.

CVCP (1988) *The British PhD*, Report of a working group, CVCP, London.

Diamond, P. (1983) 'Theoretical positions': a comparison of intending and experienced teachers' constructs, *The South Pacific Journal of Teacher Education* 11 (1), 45-53.

Diamond, P. (1985) Becoming a teacher: an altering eye, in D. Bannister (ed.) *Issues and Approaches in Personal Construct Theory*, Academic Press, London, 15-35.

Diamond, P. and Zuber-Skerritt, O. (1986) Postgraduate research: some changing personal constructs in higher education, a paper presented to the Third Annual Conference on Computer Assisted Learning in Tertiary Education, Melbourne, and published in *Higher Education Research and Development* 5 (2), 161-75.

Economic and Social Research Council (1984) *The Preparation and Supervision of Research Theses in the Social Sciences*, ESRC, London.

Eizenberg, N. (1986) Applying student learning research to practice, in J. Bowden (ed.) *Student Learning: Research into Practice*, Centre for the Study of Higher Education, University of Melbourne, Melbourne.

Elton, L. and Pope, M. (1987) Social science PhD completion rates, *Research Intelligence* 25, 3-8.

Elton, L. and Pope, M. (1989) Research supervision: the value of collegiality, *Cambridge Journal of Education* 19 (3), 267-76.

Entwistle, N. (1984) Contrasting perspectives on learning, in F. Marton et al. (eds) *The Experience of Learning*, Scottish Academic Press, Edinburgh, 1-18.

Fleming, W. and Rutherford, D. (1984) Recommendations for learning: rhetoric and reaction, *Studies in Higher Education* 9 (1), 17-26.

Gibbs, G. (1981) *Teaching Students to Learn — A Student-Centred Approach,* The Open University Press, Milton Keynes.

Glaser, B. and Strauss, A. (1967) *The Discovery of Grounded Theory*, Aldine, Chicago.

114

Gowin, D.B. (1981) *Education*, Cornell University Press, London.

Grundy, S. and Kemmis, S. (1982) Educational action research in Australia: the state of the art (an overview), in S. Kemmis (ed.) *The Action Research Reader*, Deakin University Press, Victoria, 83-97.

Habermas, J. (1974) *Theory and Practice*, Heinemann, London.

Habermas, J. (1978) *Knowledge and Human Interest* (Second Edition), Heinemann, London.

Harri-Augstein, S. and Thomas, L.F. (1979) Self-organised learning and the relativity of knowing: towards a conversational methodology, in P. Stringer and D. Bannister (eds) *Constructs of Sociality and Individuality*, Academic Press, London, 115-32.

Harris, S.V. and Zuber-Skerritt, O. (1985) Identifying the gap between institutional expectations and the needs of graduate professionals in continuing education, a paper presented to the Annual Conference of the Society for Research into Higher Education, London.

Howard, K. and Sharp, J.A. (1983) *The Management of a Research Project*, Gower, Aldershot.

Ibrahim, E.Z., McEvan, E.M. and Pitblado, R. (1980) Doctoral supervision at Sydney University, hindrance or help? *Vestes* 23, 18-22.

Kelly, G.A. (1955) *The Psychology of Personal Constructs*, Norton, New York.

Kelly, G.A. (1963) *A Theory of Personality*, Norton, New York.

Kemmis, S.(ed.) (1982) *The Action Research Reader* (Third Edition 1988), Deakin University Press, Victoria.

Kemmis, S. and McTaggart, R. (1982) *The Action Research Planner* (Third Edition 1988), Deakin University Press, Victoria.

Kevill, F.M. and Shaw, M.L.G. (1980) A repertory grid study of staff–student interactions, *Psychology Teaching* 8 (1), 29-36.

Kevill, F.M., Shaw, M. and Goodacre, E. (1982) in-service diploma course evaluation using repertory grids, *British Educational Research Journal* 8 (1), 45-56.

Knight, G.A. (1955) *The Psychology of Personal Constructs*, Norton, New York.

Knight, N. and Zuber-Skerritt, O. (1986) 'Problems and Methods in Research': a course for the beginning researcher in the social sciences, a paper presented to the Annual Conference of the Higher Education Research and Development Society of Australasia,

Auckland, NZ, and published in *Higher Education Research and Development* 5, 49-59.

Kolb, D. (1984) *Experiential Learning. Experience as The Source of Learning and Development*, Prentice-Hall, Englewood Cliffs, New Jersey.

Laurillard, D. (1984) Learning from problem-solving, in F. Marton et al. (eds) *The Experience of Learning*, Scottish Academic Press, Edinburgh, 124-43.

Leontiev, A.N. (1977) *Tätigkeit, Bewusstsein, Persönlichkeit*, Klett-Cotta, Stuttgart.

Lewin, K. (1952) *Field Theory in Social Science*, Selected Theoretical Papers edited by D. Cartright, Tavistock Publications, London.

Limerick, D. (1991) Foreword, in O. Zuber-Skerritt (ed.) *Action Research for Change and Development*, Gower-Avebury, Aldershot, Hampshire.

McGaw, B. and Lawrence, J. (1984) Developing expertise through higher education, *HERDSA News* 6 (3), 3-7.

McQualter, J.W. (1985a) Teacher knowledge. Part 1: Unstopping the dam, *The Australian Journal of Teacher Education* 10 (2), 5-12.

McQualter, J.W. (1985b) Teacher knowledge. Part 2: Personal construct theory as the basis of a methodology to study teaching, *The Australian Journal of Teacher Education* 10 (2), 13-20.

McQualter, J.W. and Warren, W.G. (1984) The personal construction of teaching and mathematics teacher education, *The Australian Journal of Teacher Education* 9 (2),1-17.

Madsen, D. (1983) *Successful Dissertations and Theses*, Jossey-Bass, San Francisco.

Martin, E. and Ramsden, P. (1985) Learning skills or skill in learning? in J. Bowden (ed.) *Student Learning: Research into Practice*, Centre for the Study of Higher Education, University of Melbourne, Melbourne.

Marton, F., Hounsell, D.J. and Entwistle, N.J. (eds) (1984) *The Experience of Learning*, Scottish Academic Press, Edinburgh.

Moses, I. (1981) Postgraduate study: supervisors, supervision and information for students, Tertiary Education Institute, University of Queensland, Brisbane.

Moses, I. (1984) Supervision of higher degrees students — problem areas and possible solutions, *Higher Education Research and Development* 3, 153-56.

Moses, I (1985a) Academic development limits and the improvement of teaching, *Higher Education*, 14, 75-100.

Moses, I. (1985b) *Supervising Postgraduates*, HERDSA Green Guides No. 3. Higher Education Research and Development Society of Australasia, Sydney.

Moss, G.D. and McMillen, D. (1980) A strategy for developing problem-solving skills in large undergraduate classes, *Studies in Higher Education* 5 (2), 161-71.

Novak, J.M. (1988) Constructively approaching education: toward a theory of practice, *International Journal of Personal Construct Psychology* 1, 169-80.

Novak, J.D. and Gowin, D.B. (1984) *Learning How To Learn*, Cambridge University Press.

Phillips, E. and Pugh, D.S. (1987) *How to Get A PhD*, Open University Press, Milton Keynes.

Pope, M.L. and Denicolo, P. (1986) Intuitive theories — a researcher's dilemma: some practical methodological implications, *British Educational Research Journal* 12 (2), 153-166.

Pope, M.L. and Keen, T.R. (1981) *Personal Construct Psychology and Education*, Academic Press, London.

Popper, K.R. (1959) *The Logic of Scientific Discovery*, Hutchinson, London.

Popper, K.R. (1969) *Conjectures and Refutations — The Growth of Scientific Knowledge*, Routledge and Kegan Paul, London.

Powles, M. (1988) *Know Your PhD Students and How to Help Them*, Centre for the Study of Higher Education, Melbourne University, Melbourne.

Powles, M. (1989a) Higher degree completion and completion times, *Higher Education Research and Development* 8 (1), 91-101.

Powles, M. (1989b) *How's the Thesis Going?* Centre for the Study of Higher Education, Melbourne University, Melbourne.

Ramsden, P. (1984) The context of learning, in F. Marton et al. (eds) *The Experience of Learning*, Scottish Academic Press, Edinburgh.

Ramsden, P. and Entwistle, N.J. (1981) Effects of academic departments on students' approaches to studying, *British Journal of Educational Psychology* 51, 368-83.

Rudd, E. (1975) *The Highest Education*, Routledge and Kegan Paul, London.

Rudd, E. (1984) Research into postgraduate education, *Higher Education Research and Development* 3, 109-20.

Rudd, E. (1985) *A New Look at Postgraduate Failure*, Society for Research into Higher Education, Guildford.

Säljö, R. (1982) *Learning and Understanding: A Study of Differences in Constructing Meaning from a Text*, Acta Universitatis Gothoburgensis, Göteborg.

Schön, A. (1983) *The Reflective Practitioner: How Professionals Think in Action*, Temple Smith, London.

Science and Engineering Research Council (1983) *Research Student and Supervisor. An Approach to Good Supervisory Practice*, SERC, London.

Shaw, M.L.G. (1980) *On Becoming a Personal Scientist: Interactive Computer Elicitation of Personal Models of the World*, Academic Press, London.

Shaw, M.L.G. (1984) *PLANET: Personal Learning, Analysis, Negotiation and Elicitation Techniques*, Department of Computer Science, York University, Ontario, Canada.

Social Science Research Council (1980) *Report: April 1979 - March 1980*, SSRC, London.

Svensson, L. (1984) Skill in learning, in F. Marton et al. (eds) *The Experience of Learning*, Scottish Academic Press, Edinburgh, 56-79.

Turney, J. (1985) ESRC cracks down on PhD rates, *Higher Education Supplement*, November 1-2, 1.

Welsh, J.M. (1979) *The First Year of Postgraduate Research Study*, SRHE Monograph, University of Surrey, Guildford.

Zuber-Skerritt, O. (1985) The use of the repertory grid technique in a study of postgraduate students' and supervisors' personal constructs of research, *Proceedings of the Sixth Australasian Tertiary Study Skills Conference*, Adelaide.

Zuber-Skerritt, O. (1986a) The integration of university student learning skills in undergraduate programmes, *Educational Training and Technology International* 24 (1), 62-70. Also published in J. Bowden (ed.) *Student Learning: Research into Practice*, CSHE, University of Melbourne, Melbourne, 115-30.

Zuber-Skerritt, O. (1986b) Developing discussion skills, in P. Cryer (ed.) *Training Activities for Teachers in Higher Education* 3, SRHE, Guildford, 77-98.

Zuber-Skerritt, O. (1987a) A repertory grid study of staff and students' personal constructs of educational research, *Higher Education* 16 (5-6), 603-23.

Zuber-Skerritt, O. (1987b) Helping postgraduate students learn, *Higher Education* 16 (1), 75-94.

Zuber-Skerritt, O. (1988) What constitutes effective research? A case study, *Higher Education in Europe* 13 (4), 64-76.

Zuber-Skerritt, O. (1989) Case study: personal constructs of second language teaching, *Educational and Training Technology International* 26 (1), 60-67.

Zuber-Skerritt, O. (1990a) The dialectical relationship between theory and practice in higher education, in C. Gellert, E. Leitner and J. Schramm (eds) *Research and Teaching at Universities — International and Comparative Perspectives*, Peter Lang, Frankfurt, 165-92.

Zuber-Skerritt, O. (1990b) Reflections of action researchers, in I. Moses (ed.) *Higher Education in the Late Twentieth Century: Reflections on a Changing System*, Higher Education Research and Development Society of Australasia, Sydney, 295-313.

Zuber-Skerritt, O. (1991) *Action Research for Change and Development*, Gower-Avebury, Aldershot, Hampshire.

Zuber-Skerritt, O. (1992) *Professional Development in Higher Education — A Theoretical Framework For Action Research*, Kogan Page, London.

Zuber-Skerritt, O. and Cunningham, D. (eds) (1986) *Student Learning Skills Guidelines*, CALT, Griffith University.

Zuber-Skerritt, O. and Knight, N. (1985) Helping students overcome barriers to dissertation writing, *HERDSA News* 7 (3), 8-10.

Zuber-Skerritt, O. and Knight, N. (1986) Problem definition and thesis writing: workshops for the postgraduate student, *Higher Education* 15, 89-103.

Zuber, O. and Marwick, M. (1976) Group-centred instead of lecturer-centred methods of tertiary learning and teaching — an experiment in teaching sociology, *The Australian Journal of Advanced Education* (June), 10-18.

Zuber-Skerritt, O. and Rix, A. (1986) Developing skills in dissertation research and writing for postgraduate coursework programmes, a paper presented to the Annual Conference of the Society for Research into Higher Education, London, and published in *Zeitschrift für Hochschuldidaktik* 10, 363-80.

# Author index

# Subject index